C000005415

Health
From East
To West

Life story of a whistle-blower

Dr Mohammad M Asghar

Edited by Dr Michael Asghar

ISBN: 9798676306182

DEDICATION

To my wife Shahnaz, who has supported me all along through difficult times

TABLE OF CONTENTS

PROLOGUE 11

A JUNIOR DOCTOR 17

RURAL LIFE 23

ISLAND LIFE... 31

IRELAND 39

THE WHISTLE-BLOWER.. 47

"WHEN HOSPITALS KILL" 55

CONSTRUCTIVE DISMISSAL... 65

EAST AND WEST 85

EPILOGUE... 95

EDITOR'S NOTE

My father is a quiet man. I have never been able to visualise him as a prototypical TV doctor, running around barking commands to nurses and junior doctors, "I need a crash cart, stat!" Then again, perhaps I watch too much TV. Regardless, "my dad is a doctor" has been a refrain I've repeated for my entire life, and I can confirm that I have seen this calm, cautious and generally treacle-like human being roam around wards in various hospitals. The realisation that your parent has a different persona outside of the father-son relationship is jarring, to say the least. What upended the jar and smashed it on the floor was when I started to read the text you are holding in your hands. Quiet he is, seemingly, only auditorily speaking.

I have managed to inherit my dad's shadowy and tranquil personality, albeit only on the exterior. Within, my mother's anxiety and short temper boil and bubble venomously. The result of this is an emotional rollercoaster; just ask my wife. My patience was wearing thin when one evening, my now retired, white-haired father spoke to me in one of our few, "serious" exchanges.

"I'm writing a book," he said.

I believe my reply was, "Mmh."

"I'd like you to edit it for me." I groaned aloud. Yes, I know, I'm an ungrateful, spoiled brat.

A few weeks passed, the manuscript sitting idly in its green folder, atop a box of my child's toys. This was January 2020. The calm before the storm, some will say in future history books. 2020 has been chaotic, and that's underselling it. I'm writing this during a global pandemic instigated by COVID-19; a highly infectious strain of coronavirus. My regular University work has been put on pause, and along with my wife, we have spent most of our time looking after a 2-year-old and a new-born. I am ashamed to say that I ignored my father's work for a long time. The evenings were spent in TV-induced stupors or coma-like video game marathons. Finally, one hot and stormy evening, I sat down and opened up the folder. Inside I found newspaper clippings, hospital reports, letters, photographs and a 50-ish page manuscript; I read the entire thing in one sitting. It was at this point that I started to understand my otherwise mute father.

*

As a citizen of the United Kingdom, I have used the NHS uncountable times. I am forever thankful that I live in a country where an excellent health service is provided for free. My experience, on the patient side at least, has been nothing short of satisfactory. I have a good GP, and my various waits in A&E's haven't been too torturous. A fractured arm in Barrow-in-Furness, a lacerated finger in Manchester, or even being hospitalised with meningitis in Northern Ireland; I came out of these maladies positively, thanks to the NHS.

After reading my father's text, I now have a second-hand experience of the difficult workplace politics that are embroiled in our healthcare system. At the time, I had no idea of the stress and depression my father went through, expressed only by his silence. The skeletons in hospital closets are being unveiled, day by day. Better scrutiny and oversight mean that hospitals are becoming more transparent, however, preventable deaths follow the NHS around like a shadowy spectre. In this text, my father explicitly describes two such events, which led to two large investigations; the hyponatremia child deaths in Northern Ireland, and the failings of a former maternity unit in Morecambe Bay, UK. My father's perspective on these is at times difficult to read, and from my reading, he happened to just be doing his job and was in the wrong place at the wrong time. My father refused to stay silent and went through the normal channels of voicing his concerns, however, his words fell on deaf ears.

Reading and editing this text has worried me. I hope that my family or myself are not one of the patients that fall through the gaps in the paperwork. When you or your loved ones are ill, you delegate control to the doctor, to the hospital. There are more qualified people than you to look after them. This comes with an unspoken contract of trust; that they will receive the best possible care. In the back of my head now, however, I feel an itch, "-but will they?"

I've learned that the capacity to empathise and the ability to listen and communicate effectively are some of the most important traits for any career, and for any relationship for that matter. My father describes a journey from rural Pakistan, where treating simple procedures can be a matter of life and death, to the urbanised west, with advanced facilities, and high levels of education. The twist, or the sting, comes in the form of excessive middle management, target-hitting, and selfishness. In some cases, empathy is merely a veneer, skin-deep. I can only hope that hospitals continue to improve, and that cover-ups and cultures of fear disappear from our health system.

*

My father has retired now, living out his best life by the sea, caring only about booking tennis courts and visiting his grandchildren - rightly so. On a recent trip I started to see some chips in his concrete demeanour break off and dissolve. Perhaps then, writing this, was a cathartic experience. I hope that now he can put his mind at rest and know that I've tried my best to form a cohesive story, without losing his voice in the process.

PROLOGUE

This is not an autobiography. It is a journey of desire, determination, dedication and devotion punctuated by disappointment and dismay.

My story starts at high school, when I was living with my uncle, an engineer with WAPDA (Water and Power Development Authority), in Pakistan. I used to visit his office often and perhaps subconsciously or unintentionally I was heading towards a career in engineering. I was a diligent student in school and regularly achieved high grades in every subject. A flair for drawing and architecture led me to continue the subject at A Level.

Unfortunately (or perhaps fortunately) our drawing teacher suddenly resigned and left the school. The headmaster came to our class and ordered all those studying drawing and architecture to join the medical physiology class.

After a few months a new drawing teacher was appointed and all displaced students resumed their former studies, except me. The physiology teacher asked me whether I was sure I wanted to continue with physiology; I was positive. I found human anatomy and physiology so compelling that even after joining the class late into the syllabus I received top grades in the next test.

This was the start of my pre-medical journey.

*

There are a few things you never forget in life, as if they happened only yesterday.

I vividly remember my teacher asking me to write a short essay on a topic of my choice. I have forgotten the content of the essay, but I do recall that when I read it aloud, he said something that is forever ingrained in my memory: "I do not know what you will become, whether an engineer, teacher, or lawyer. But I do know one thing, that you will certainly be a writer".

Something I will never forget is our father telling my brother and sisters and I that he didn't have any land or money to give, but he would give us an education. He paid our university fees despite financial difficulties and supported us until we graduated.

These memories were the first steps towards me becoming a medical doctor and writing this book.

*

As a junior doctor I was taught and trained to make sure that the basic principles of treatment (ABCD) are adhered to as follows:

1. Airway
2. Breathing
3. Circulation
4. Drugs/disability

But after working in the UK National Health Service for twenty-five years, I have discovered that there might be another meaning to ABCD as follows:

1. Allegation
2. Blame and bullying culture
3. Cover-up
4. Detriment

This book is an account of my journey starting from my qualification as a doctor and my vocation and desire to serve patients to the best of my ability, all the while coming across obstacles, political interests, power struggle, selfishness, mismanagement of resources and my struggles and endeavour to set things right and alleviate people's suffering. After forty-five years of my medical professional life I have learnt that even if you are an honest and hard working person devoted to your profession, it <u>does not mean</u> that life is going to be smooth sailing and that you are not going to face any difficulties in your professional life.

This is my story.

A JUNIOR DOCTOR

A JUNIOR DOCTOR

Getting into medical college in Pakistan was not easy; admissions were strictly on a merit basis. Moving from the Urdu medium of instruction at GCSE level (General Certificate of Secondary Education) to English at A Level was a shock to me and perhaps to many other classmates. I didn't achieve high grades and therefore didn't get into medical college. I decided to do an undergraduate bachelor's degree and was determined to work hard and reapply; and I did. I was called up for an interview at King Edward Medical University, Lahore; one of the oldest and most respected medical institutions for education and training. Following the interview, a clerk looked at my file and mumbled to the panel, who nodded their heads. After a few minutes I was told that I was not eligible for admission. I was crushed.

Sometimes unexpected things can happen that change your entire life. My close friend, who had been my classmate in school and was in his first year at King Edward, was standing outside waiting for me to tell him how the interview went. I told him the result and he was extremely disappointed. During this conversation, I overheard another candidate talking to his relatives that even though he didn't achieve high grades at A Level he was still admitted on the basis of being from a rural area in Jhelum. I was shocked as I had higher grades and had also applied from the same rural district. My friend told me to go back in the office and speak to the interview panel. I knocked on the door and we both went in. I explained that I had higher grades while another candidate with lower grades had been selected from the same district. The same clerk looked at the file again and said, "Sorry there has been a typing mistake". He apologised and handed me the admission forms. Had I not overheard that conversation, the typo would never have been discovered and I would have never been admitted to the medical college and may never have become a doctor.

Five years at medical college was all hard work and intense study, but I found some time to write short stories and poems, being interested in Urdu literature. I was appointed editor for the college magazine, KEMCOL, (King Edward Medical College of Lahore). When I qualified as a doctor, I came in the top 20 out of 160 students; the incentive here was that only those who qualified top of the class would get a paid job, "house job" (residency) in the Mayo hospital; one of the tertiary medical centres in Pakistan. The rest of the students would apply for other jobs in the private sector or embark on a year of voluntary (honorary) work in hospitals to get experience. I managed to get my one year of residency in the neurosurgery department as a junior house surgeon. My salary was 250 rupees/month (approximately £5 in 1973). I would usually give 150 rupees to my parents and keep the rest for my monthly expenses. However, tough times were ahead.

*

The neurosurgery department was situated in a district general hospital about twenty miles away from the main hospital in Lahore. One of my classmates was also working in the neurosurgery department as a senior house surgeon. We were given a room in the hospital and were told to bring our own beds. An ambulance was sent to my home where I loaded up my suitcase, bed, sheets, and a pillow.

The team at the neurosurgery department comprised two consultants, one senior and two regular registrars, two medical officers and two of us graduates as junior doctors. The unit was extremely busy. We used to get road traffic accident patients with head injuries almost every day in addition to elective admissions, e.g. patients with brain tumours, spinal cord problems, such as disc prolapses, spina-bifida, meningoceles, patients with trigeminal neuralgia and Parkinsonism for surgical intervention.

There were two elective operation days in addition to emergency operations mainly for head injuries. I remember assisting the consultant neurosurgeons for brain tumours for five to six hours at the operation table. These were long and complicated operations involving craniotomies (opening up the skull) and removing the tumours. Post-operative days were also very busy; looking after unconscious patients day and night. The mortality rate was very high.

I still remember one day a medical officer came to the doctor's office crying. I asked what happened. She said that she was going to do a lumbar puncture (where a needle is inserted into your spinal canal to collect cerebrospinal fluid) on a young boy and he was begging the doctor not to proceed, fearing his death. She reassured him that it was only a simple procedure and went ahead. Unfortunately, the boy died shortly afterwards; this was extremely distressing for us. As a young doctor, when there are seriously ill patients who are dying so often with no support for the doctors and nursing staff, I wondered whether I really wanted to become a surgeon.

The department was very chaotic. There was no defined rota. All of us worked during the day but night duties were left solely for us two junior doctors. As a rule, it should have been alternate nights for me but my colleague either used to disappear or go home twenty miles away and most of the time I ended up doing night duties almost continuously. I sometimes got a few hours' sleep in the doctor's office whenever it was comparatively quieter. The only month when I had a good night's sleep was when a nurse was on night duty and my colleague, who had a romantic interest in her, told me that he would happily do night duties for the whole month.

Now that I look back, it's hard to imagine that in a district general hospital with a tertiary neurosurgery unit there was no staff restaurant or a dining room, but I suppose that was considered the norm. Nobody ever questioned or raised this issue to management. There were a few dingy restaurants around the hospital where sometimes we used to go for an evening meal. Sometimes a porter in the hospital would make some samosas or pakoras (deep-fried, savoury pastries) for lunch with tea. Otherwise my colleague and I arranged to have meals from the nursing hostel. Irregular meals, poor nutrition, lack of sleep and an exhausting working pattern took its toll on me. I lost weight. My ankles became swollen due to long hours of standing at the operation table. However, I did learn important basic surgical procedures.

Nobody taught us the importance of communication skills, as there was no system in place requiring doctors to explain to patients what was wrong with them and why they needed a particular form of treatment. There was no concept of asking for written consent from the patients. The patients trusted the doctors whatever they were doing, and doctors didn't feel that it was necessary to involve patients in any decision-making process. None of these skills were part of the curriculum. These luxuries of life were completely unknown to anybody. As a recently qualified young doctor I was facing the stark reality of life: in a developing country, the health service depends on limited resources. You try your best for the patients but there are other factors which can affect patient care. The lack of communication between doctors and patients can lead to misunderstandings, augmented by illiteracy, low public education and general levels of understanding, resulting in a lack of trust between medical staff and patients. I have seen doctors becoming visibly angry with the patients and their relatives, and at times seen relatives verbally abusing the medical staff. Sometimes relatives of patients had physically beaten the doctors out of frustration. Angry exchanges between doctors and patients were a regular occurrence.

A year later, after finishing my residency, I was appointed as a medical officer in another city for 700 rupees/month. Our family had always lived in rented accommodation. My father had expected that once I become a doctor, I would earn a lot of money and should be able to help the family; I'm sure he was disappointed. Considering the financial situation of my family I decided to go abroad, having heard good things about making money elsewhere in the Middle East. I applied to the Ministry of Health, Iran and was soon accepted as a medical officer. The next stage of my medical adventure beckoned.

RURAL LIFE

At Lahore airport, my parents, brother and sisters came to say goodbye. I landed in Tehran with a group of doctors and was appointed to work in the southern province of Bandar Abbas; a seaport in the hottest part of the country where temperatures can reach 45-50 °C.

The Director General sent me to work in a remote rural health centre about six hours journey by Land Rover from the city. The road was crumbling and muddy with potholes, creating the effect of being in a rollercoaster. My body was shaking with such force - I was shocked at how, in such an oil-rich country, there were still heavily impoverished areas. I was accompanied by a health ministry official and we arrived in Deh Tul - a small rural health centre with five or six surrounding villages and a small town nearby. At the health centre there were two paramedics, a driver and a cleaner who was also the chef. The water supply was from a well in the building. There was no mains electricity; only a generator which was put on at night for a few hours.

I started working as a medical officer but soon realised that I was in fact a physician, a surgeon doing minor surgical procedures, paediatrician and obstetrician/gynaecologist all at once. As a doctor working in remote rural areas you do the best you can for your patients with whatever limited resources are available. There are no guidelines, auditing or targets. You rely on your own knowledge and experience to serve and treat patients; and that's what I did. At the same time, you feel part of the community. I soon became acquainted with local people and the "Kadkhuda" (local chief) of the village. I used to attend the local mosque for Friday prayers. People in the area used to invite us for tea, evening meals or even weddings.

Every few months I travelled to the ministry of health in Bandar Abbas for official work. During monsoon season the previously mentioned muddy roads would disappear. Once when travelling to the city we lost our way at night. The Land Rover stopped, and the engine wouldn't start even after the paramedic and I got out and started pushing the car. I ended up sleeping on the car's backseat while the driver and paramedic slept on the roof. In the morning we were luckily rescued by a helicopter; the pilot had spotted us stuck in the desert.

One day a man came to the health centre and told me that his wife was delivering, and the baby was "stuck". I took my medical bag, got in the Rover along with the paramedic and drove quickly to the village, about thirty minutes away. When we arrived at the house the man ushered us into a room where his wife was in labour. There was an old woman sitting beside her. She lifted the sheet and I received the shock of my life. I was horrified to see the baby hanging from the vaginal orifice with the head still in the birth canal; it was a breech delivery. The body of the baby had gone pale/ashen grey. There was no midwife in the area; only the old women conducted the deliveries. All they knew was to cut and tie the umbilical cord after the baby was born. From my obstetric knowledge and training in the final year of medical college I used the Mauriceau-Smellie-Veit [1] manoeuvre to extract the baby. Unfortunately, the baby had died a few hours ago when its head couldn't come out without assistance. Everybody in the room was crying except for the baby.

Another time a man was brought in experiencing a severe asthma attack. In spite of giving him bronchodilators and steroids he didn't improve. He needed oxygen which was not available in our rural remote health centre. He needed to be ventilated but when there were no basic facilities or even basic medicine, the

---

[1] A specialist, invasive technique where the obstetrician inserts his/her hand into the vagina, attempting to safely pull the breeched baby out, applying neck flexion, traction towards the pelvis, and suprapubic pressure.

concept of intensive care was non-existent. When you are living in a remote rural area you live life on a knife-edge. If you become seriously ill your chances of survival are very slim. All a doctor can do is to use whatever sort of treatment is available and pray.

One day a man came over and asked me if I could go to a nearby village to help out at an emergency. After we drove a little bit, we came to an impasse. We were told that from here on we would need to go up the mountain on foot as there was no useable road. After walking for about half an hour up the hills, I saw a small house with a few trees around. We sat down outside the house on carpets. A pregnant woman who was probably the man's wife brought some tea and dates. After a while the man said, "Please come in and see my wife and check if the baby is okay". I then realised that this was the "emergency" for which we were called in. I examined his wife, listened to the baby's heartbeat and reassured them that the baby was fine.

We received a letter from the ministry of health that there had been an epidemic of measles in a nearby village and I was asked to go there and vaccinate the children. I was not sure how effective that would be as the other children would have already contracted the disease. But the village chief had written to the ministry and he wanted the children to be vaccinated - I had no choice, the director general of the health ministry would not listen to me. We drove to the nearest village. Upon arrival, the village chief told us that the car could not go any further as the affected village was high up in the mountains (a common occurrence as you can see). He told us that we would have to leave tomorrow early in the morning. I thought perhaps we would be sent there by helicopter. In the morning we walked down the path and saw three donkeys at the bottom of the village; one for me, one for the paramedic and one for the guide. I was helped to sit on the donkey.

The guide told me to hold the reins and said, "If you pull the right rein the donkey will start walking. This is the accelerator. If you pull the left rein the donkey will stop. This is the brake."

I asked drily, "If this is the accelerator, and the other one is the brake, then where is the clutch?"

The guide said, "Doctor, there is no clutch in this vehicle. It's an automatic".

We arrived in the village riding on the donkeys and vaccinated the children, stayed overnight and ended up eating some dirty kebabs.

LIFE IN REMOTE RURAL AREAS

ISLAND LIFE

Qeshm Island is about half an hour from Bandar Abbas by boat through the Strait of Hormoz, a strategic body of water where tankers from oil rich countries like Saudi Arabia, Qatar, Kuwait and Bahrain pass through.

There are many pros and cons to living on an island. A good thing is that you get to know the locals very soon. A bad thing is that you are isolated.

In Qeshm there were four health centres; all were managed by non-Iranian doctors as the local doctors did not want to work in remote areas on the island. The centres operated as out-patient departments with no facilities for seriously ill patients and were isolated and disconnected from the main land hospital, literally, insofar that there wasn't even a telephone line, as well as no direct line to the ministry of health in Bandar Abbas. The sick patients needed to be transferred to the mainland hospital by boat at one's own expense. The situation became worse in winter, when for a week or so, severe weather prevented any boats sailing to the mainland. The infrastructure of the health system in the southern part of Iran was uncertain, while those living in the north of country, near Tehran and other big cities, enjoyed better facilities.

Transferring seriously ill patients to the mainland hospital was problematic. I still remember a man who was brought into the health centre after a gas cylinder exploded and hit him on the head. He had a deep, six-inch long wound that split his face in two from forehead to chin, bleeding profusely. We stitched and stopping the bleeding, gave intravenous fluid etc., but he needed immediate transfer to the mainland for admission with continued care. I contacted the hospital from the governor's office and found it extremely difficult to convince the consultant that this man with a severe head injury needed immediate transfer. I told him about the urgency of the situation, describing his injuries but he kept asking me to go back and check his pupils. I knew from my neurosurgery experience that any delay could be fatal and if the pupils became unequal sizes, he would need immediate burr holes (holes drilled into the skull) and evacuation of any haematoma. The patient was finally transferred by a private boat to the mainland hospital, but he later unfortunately died.

One evening a teenage boy was brought in with severe burns after his motorcycle caught fire. All that could be done was to apply bandages and give him intravenous fluid. He was forced to wait until morning before he could be transferred to the mainland hospital.

One afternoon five or six injured patients were brought in after a two-vehicle collision. They needed immediate treatment with suturing wounds, intravenous fluid and resuscitation. I had to call for additional staff from the nearby health centre ten miles away. Two doctors and paramedics rushed in and we were able to manage the casualties. Luckily, all of them survived.

A woman in labour was diagnosed with eclampsia and needed to be transferred for immediate Caesarean section. When I arrived, there were two other doctors already present. The woman was having frequent convulsions/seizures with labour pains. She was transferred by boat accompanied by a midwife. The time of day saved her since it was morning; boats were ready to sail, so there was no delay in transferring her. It would have been a different story if she had to be transferred to the mainland at night. This was impossible as no boat was equipped to sail at night, nor would helicopters make the crossing.

*

I wrote to the director general of the ministry of health and governor of the island about all these problems for urgent action. This is a summary of my suggestions:

1. There needs to be a direct telephone connection with the mainland hospital to discuss seriously ill patients for advice, management and their transfer.

2. Transferring seriously ill patients is of paramount importance with a robust system of transfer essential, particularly when seas are rough in severe weather. Helicopter transfer is the only solution.

3. There is an urgent need for a four-to-six bedded small hospital on the island where patients could be admitted prior to transfer.

There was no response from the governor, but the director general agreed with my points and soon an ambulance with a wireless connection was dispatched to the island as a crude temporary measure.

Soon after my recommendations, I received a letter from the health ministry for my immediate relocation to a city in Iran: Shiraz. I was undoubtedly perceived as a troublemaker. I was appointed in a district general hospital in Shiraz as a casualty medical officer. Patient care was, however, no different to Qeshm island.

I remember when four patients were brought in with severe injuries after an RTA (road traffic accident). The porters lifted one patient from the stretcher by holding his arms and legs with his back sagging. Suddenly he collapsed and died.

Another patient was so irritable and agitated that the surgeon decided to give him intravenous diazepam. He gave the injection so fast that the patient went into respiratory depression. He stopped breathing and was never resuscitated. Had he been ventilated immediately he might have survived an avoidable death.

There was no concept of teaching; no structured lessons on how to deal with seriously injured patients, resuscitation and stabilisation, airway management in cervical spine injury, rolling and lifting patients in a safe way, etc.

Additionally, there was never any thorough investigation into patient deaths. Doctors didn't have to be a member of a medical defence union (an organisation that provides legal support should a doctor's clinical competence be questioned). Everything was black and white: if the patient survived and recovered, the doctor was good. If the patient died it was "God's wish".

I made the decision to receive higher education and further medical training, to serve patients to the highest standards. I wrote to University College Dublin for a diploma in child health and was accepted.

QHESM ISLAND TEAM

WORKING HARD

PARTYING HARD

IRELAND

On 29th of September 1981 I landed in Dublin airport. A taxi trip transported me to a hotel in the city, late at night. The driver dropped me off at a Bed and Breakfast near O'Connell street. The taxi fare was £5. I only had English currency with me and gave him a £10 note. The driver was apprehensive, presumably thinking that I didn't know that the Irish currency was weaker[2] than Sterling. He quickly gave me the change and drove away.

---

[2]In the '70s, the Irish pound had a fixed link with English Sterling, but the introduction of the European Exchange Rate Mechanism sought to reduce exchange rate variability and improve monetary stability across

I was given a room and slept well after a long flight. Coming from an eastern country to the west was a culture shock. I rose in the morning and went to the breakfast room. The landlady came over and asked me if I wanted a "full Irish". To save face, not knowing what I was agreeing to, I said yes. Ten minutes later, she brought me a hot, greasy plate of toast, fried eggs, baked beans, grilled tomatoes, mushrooms, hash browns (fried potatoes), and some meat I had never seen before (sausages and bacon). I was not accustomed to such a heavy breakfast, but I enjoyed it. Later, however, I was appalled to discover that the sausages and bacon were pork, and having been raised Muslim, I was aghast.

From then on, I had to be careful what I ate. I went to the tourist office where people were very helpful and the receptionist found me a room in a private home as a paying guest in the suburb of Raheny, north of Dublin. This was obviously much cheaper than staying in a hotel. There was another person staying in the same house, who was from Saudi Arabia and had come over to Ireland to learn English. The first question he asked me was, "Have you bought an umbrella?" I curiously replied no, and he explained that here, you can't leave the house without an umbrella, "In Ireland there are only two seasons: rain, and heavy rain."

*

countries in the European Economic Community. While the Euro didn't come into circulation until 2002, in 1979, the 1-to-1 link of the Irish pound to Sterling was broken by an exchange rate system.

I was doing a course in child health in Our Lady's Hospital, Crumlin. The hospital was situated south of Dublin and I had to travel by bus through the city centre. The landlady told me that it would be more convenient and cost effective if I lived in the south, so I had to move again.

The course itself was very interesting and I learned a lot. I passed and decided to stay in Ireland to gain experience in paediatrics. The medical progression system was very different from eastern countries. I applied for paediatric jobs in different hospitals over a period of six months. In the medical system, to progress in those times in Ireland, once you are employed for six months you soon start looking for the next thing. The big problem was to get a job in paediatrics as this was a very popular speciality. The rule in Ireland was that Irish nationals had first priority for the job, then EU nationals and only after that, doctors from overseas would be considered. Despite this, I managed to get my foot in the paediatric door and received my MRCPI (Membership of Royal College of Physicians of Ireland). There was, however, a period of time where I remained unemployed. During these periods I studied and attended different courses and took exams. I received a diploma in child health, in tropical medicine, the MRCPCH (Membership of Royal College of Paediatrics and Child Health) from London and then a FRCPCH (Fellowship of Royal College of Paediatrics and Child health). I was engaged in research and managed to publish a few papers.

*

I worked in different hospitals all over the country for ten years, gaining experience in general and neonatal paediatrics. I found the consultants and colleagues very friendly and helpful. I really felt comfortable and at home with them; I never wanted to leave Ireland.

Patients understood and appreciated what a doctor was doing for them. This was in total contrast to working in an eastern country. I worked up to 130 hours/week, sometimes continuously without a break over the weekends. It was tiring but worth it. I learned how to communicate with patients and their relatives and how to treat them with dignity – this was incredibly important.

*

While I was highly qualified by this time, I still struggled to secure a consultant post because of the limited opportunities in the Republic. Subsequently, I decided to move north, a lot further north, to Northern Ireland. Life in Northern Ireland was not the same as in the south. The religious divide between two sects of Christianity; Catholics and Protestants, was bubbling under the surface in the early '90s. During the marching season in July there were often clashes between the two groups with the RUC (Royal Ulster Constabulary) trying to keep them apart. The political scene with IRA, Sinn Fein, Ulster Unionists and other political parties was a tinderbox, compared to the chilled-out stability in the Republic.

RECEIVING MRCPI IN PAEDIATRICS AT THE ROYAL COLLEGE OF
DUBLIN

THE WHISTLE-BLOWER

In 1995 I moved to Northern Ireland. I was appointed in Erne hospital, Enniskillen. This was a small district general hospital (DGH). The paediatric department consisted of a twenty-bedded children's ward and a newly opened level one neonatal unit. The neonatal unit was opened after the children's ward and the maternity unit were closed in Omagh Hospital; thirty miles north-east. Geographically, the DGH in Omagh was situated midway between Enniskillen and Londonderry (far north of Enniskillen). Altnagelvin hospital, situated two miles away from Londonderry, also incorporated a children ward's and a neonatal unit. As there was no neonatal unit in the west of Northern Ireland, it was suggested that if the paediatric services and the maternity unit were closed in Omagh and a neonatal unit opened in Enniskillen, it would serve the whole western Northern Irish population. However, this did not go to plan, as for some reason women from Omagh preferred to go to Altnagelvin hospital rather than come to Enniskillen for deliveries. Adding to this mystery was my observation that prior to the neonatal unit opening in Enniskillen, the paediatric ward was being looked after by a physician, not a paediatrician. I was surprised by the care the paediatric population was being given in western Northern Ireland, while just across the border in the Republic, where I had been working for more than ten years, paediatric care was excellent. It seemed as if I had moved to a developing country.

A general paediatrician was appointed just before I moved to Erne Hospital. He had spent most of his life working in hospitals in Africa. He was very kind, hardworking and very helpful but he was not a neonatologist. The opening of a neonatal unit without a trained neonatologist had its own problems.

I remember the day when I was called to theatre where a caesarean section was planned. I scrubbed up and went to the theatre, checked for oxygen, suction, overhead heating and other equipment. There was no neonatal laryngoscope[3]. There were only adult laryngoscopes with large blades. I asked the theatre sister about the neonatal laryngoscope. The answer was, "we have

---

[3] A viewing instrument used for endoscopy of the larynx, e.g. for intubation

always used these". The baby was born but was late to cry. I started bagging the baby[4] and asked the nurse to prepare for intubation. Somebody rang the neonatal unit and I saw a nurse running into theatre; she had brought a neonatal laryngoscope from the unit. Thankfully the baby started crying, so we didn't need it in the end. I discussed the lack of proper neonatal equipment in theatre with the lead consultant paediatrician. His answer was, "we are waiting for a neonatologist to be appointed". After a few uneasy months a paediatrician with neonatal experience was finally appointed.

After a while another paediatrician was appointed who held clinics. Soon after his appointment we began to hear concerns regarding his clinical practice. I did not know the exact nature of those concerns but after some time a meeting was arranged between him, the chief executive and the lead paediatrician and he was suspended from his work in the community. He confined his practice to general paediatrics and neonatology. However, problems started emerging on this front as well.

A five-year-old child was admitted with congenital adrenal hypoplasia[5] over a bank holiday weekend. When I came back to the ward after the weekend, a junior doctor informed me that the child had low sodium over the weekend. I was alarmed to see the child lying untreated on the ward. A child with adrenal

---

[4] Pump air into the baby's lungs using oxygen and a rubber bag to assist breathing

[5] A genetic metabolic disorder that affects the production of sex steroids and primary and secondary sex characteristics

insufficiency developing hyponatraemia[6] is an emergency and needs to be treated with steroids immediately. I quickly picked up the phone and discussed the case with the consultant endocrinologist in a tertiary centre in Belfast. She told me that the child who had been lying on the ward with hyponatraemia untreated over the weekend could have died and advised me to commence him on steroids immediately. I informed the consultant who was on-call over the weekend (the same doctor who had been suspended from his community work). He agreed and phoned the pharmacy. When he realised his mistake, he came to my office and tried to blame me for the oversight. He asked why *I* didn't start the child on steroids over the weekend. I told him that I wasn't working over the weekend and it was himself who had not checked the results and had not commenced the child on steroids. It soon became apparent to me that he had a bullying and blaming attitude to all his work.

This child was later investigated and was found to have contiguous gene deletion syndrome involving glycerol kinase deficiency and Duchenne muscular dystrophy loci. I wrote a case report about him which was later published in the Journal of Inherited Metabolic Disease.

---

[6] Low sodium concentration in the blood that can lead to death if untreated

51

J. Inher. Metab. Dis. 22 (1999) 933–935
© SSIEM and Kluwer Academic Publishers. Printed in the Netherlands

CASE REPORT

Contiguous gene deletion syndrome involving glycerol kinase and Duchenne muscular dystrophy loci

M. Asghar[1]*, N. C. Nevin*[2], *E. D. Beattie*[2], *D. McManus*[2], *G. M. A. Roberts*[3] *and J. A. Phillips*[1]

[1] Department of Paediatrics, Erne Hospital, Enniskillen; [2] Northern Ireland Regional Genetics Centre, Belfast City Hospital Trust, Belfast; [3] Department of Clinical Biochemistry, Royal Victoria Hospital, Belfast, N. Ireland
* Correspondence: Department of Paediatrics, Erne Hospital, Enniskillen, N. Ireland, BT74 6AY

The association between Duchenne muscular dystrophy (DMD), congenital adrenal hypoplasia, mental retardation and glycerol kinase deficiency (GKD) (McKusick 307030) is well recognized (Chelly et al 1988; Franke et al 1987). Affected individuals have deletions of variable size around the Duchenne muscular dystrophy locus (Xp21). We report a child who presented with failure to thrive and was found to have glycerol kinase (GK) (EC 2.7.130) deficiency and Duchenne muscular dystrophy due to a deletion of Xp21.2.

The child was born to a primigravida mother by elective Caesarean section because of breech presentation at term. Birth weight was 2900 g (3rd centile) with good Apgar score. At age 1 month he was referred by the health visitor because he was not thriving. His weight had fallen significantly below the third centile. Clinical examination was normal; in particular he had no dysmorphic features. An ultrasound of brain showed mild generalized ventricular dilatation. At 7 weeks of age he was not smiling or fixing to bright lights. There was no optokinetic nystagmus, but fundi were normal. He was considered to have delayed visual maturation. Evoked potential recording showed no evidence of hearing loss.

Investigation of urine revealed a grossly increased excretion of glycerol. The creatine kinase was elevated to 3371 and 3823 U/L (reference range 30–140) and lactate dehydrogenase to 1729 and 1926 U/L (reference range 360–720). Cortisol levels and orotic acid excretion were normal.

A skin biopsy was performed and fibroblast culture was established. [^{14}C]Glycerol incorporation into fibroblast protein was measured and was 0.5 pmol/mg protein per 24 h (control ($n = 4$) 35–99), confirming glycerol kinase deficiency. G-banded chromosome analysis showed a small interstitial deletion in the short arm of the X-chromosome. The karyotype was 46,XY,del (X)(pter → p21.3 : :p21.1 → qter). PCR screening for 21 exons of the dystrophin gene showed an apparent deletion of all exons, indicating a deletion involving the entire muscular dystrophy (DMD) locus. Chromosome analysis of the patient's mother (Figure 1; III.2) shows that she has a similar deletion to that of her son.

Glycerol kinase deficiency (GK) may occur as an isolated abnormality or as part

CASE REPORT

52

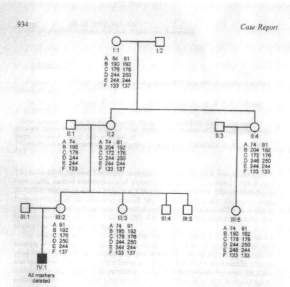

Figure 1   Pedigree of the family. A, B, C, D, E, F represents markers DYS 11, STR 44, STR 45, STR 50, and 3'CA, respectively, with the DMD locus. IV,1 the affected patient, is deleted for all markers at the DMD locus. The mother, III,2 is also deleted for all the markers, confirming her carrier status. She has inherited this X-chromosome from her father II,1. Her sister, III,3, who has a normal paternal haplotype, has not inherited the microdeletion and thus is not a carrier

of a contiguous gene deletion syndrome involving DMD, adrenal hypoplasia and glycerol kinase loci. Our patient has deletion involving the glycerol kinase and DMD genes confirmed by cytogenetics and molecular studies. Patients with the adrenal hypoplasia–mental retardation–muscular dystrophy syndrome may present with recurrent episodes of vomiting, metabolic acidosis, ketonuria, hyperglycerolaemia and glyceroluria. The involvement of the DMD locus will result in progressive muscular dystrophy (McCabe 1995). Our patient has deletion of the whole DMD gene. He is also developmentally delayed and at 21 months he has just started sitting, but is not weight bearing and is unable to crawl or walk.

Other suspect cases include a child that was admitted with Kawasaki disease with clear diagnostic signs, but he was not treated with immunoglobulin, the team falsely thinking it was a regular viral infection.

Another ten-year-old girl was being seen in the outpatient's department with classic signs of a space occupying brain lesion. She was being incorrectly treated for sinusitis for six months until a final diagnosis was made by an ENT (ear-nose-throat) consultant of the brain tumour.

Overall, I reported ~ten children who were misdiagnosed with regard to their diagnosis and management. I wrote to the lead consultant, clinical and medical director, chairman of the consultant committee and the chief executive. Nobody answered. Everybody remained silent. This continued until disaster struck.

*

A seven-year-old girl was admitted with gastroenteritis, with symptoms of vomiting and diarrhoea. She was commenced on intravenous fluid. Sometime during the night, the girl experienced convulsions and collapsed. The same, error-prone consultant was on-call and was called in. The girl needed ventilation and was transferred to the Royal Hospital in Belfast but unfortunately died. An investigation showed that she had been given an excessive amount of fluid and she died of hyponatraemia causing coning[7] of brain. I vividly remember the consultant writing in her notes

---

[7] Brain herniation, a deadly side effect of high pressure within the skull

after her death that he had ordered the fluid to be given at 30 ml/hour. A few days later I saw a junior doctor who was on-call that night and was involved in her treatment, leaving his office very upset. He informed me that the consultant had told him that "I can put the blame on you, but I won't do it." Additionally, the consultant told him that if he wants to write something in the notes, he can do it. I advised him strongly not to add or alter the notes. I felt so sad and devastated how a senior doctor could try to cover up his own negligence.

I had a meeting with the medical director and told him that if my concerns were not investigated, I would write to the GMC (General Medical Council). The director finally contacted the Royal College of Paediatrics in London. Someone came down and investigated, interviewing all the relevant staff and submitted a report. I was never informed about the outcome, but I heard from a colleague that in summary the conclusion was a "personality clash" between myself and the negligent consultant. I was confused how somebody at such a senior level would not be able to see the incompetency of a consultant. How could it be so easy to remain silent and let patients suffer and die?

"WHEN HOSPITALS KILL"

The investigation took a turn. The case of the child who had died from excess fluid and hyponatraemia was referred to the MPTS (Medical Practitioner Tribunal Service) in Manchester. This was reported in the local newspaper, *The Impartial Reporter*.

Sometime after this investigation, when I had moved to England, I heard that the consultant involved was referred again to MPTS due to further concerns and he was struck off the GMC register.

When I had sent letters to all the relevant people in the Trust, he had obviously become aware that I had reported him. The working atmosphere in the department deteriorated further. Two more locum consultants were employed to run the department efficiently. However, the blame culture and bullying continued. I finally decided to resign and move to England.

*

While I was still working in Northern Ireland, I received a phone call from the Belfast Television Channel. The person told me that his team was making a programme about all the children who had unfortunately died or suffered significant harm due to mismanagement while in hospital in Northern Ireland. The show was called *When Hospitals Kill* and, as I had reported a few children, the TV team would like to interview me over the phone. It's still a mystery to me how they came to know that I had reported some children and that one of them had died from hyponatraemia. Nevertheless, I spoke to the person at length, confirming my reports.

The next day, after I had finished the day's work and was sitting in my flat, somebody knocked at the door. I opened the door and to my surprise it was the Belfast Television crew at the door. There were two gentlemen and a lady. I asked them to come in and they told me they wanted me to be in the show. They were gathering information about the children who had died from hyponatraemia while being treated in other hospitals. The gentleman from the TV channel told me that they intended to talk to me about the girl who was admitted in Erne hospital with gastroenteritis and developed hyponatraemia due to receiving an excess of fluid - she had had convulsions and had died of cerebral oedema. They told me that there had been two other children who had died in similar circumstances, one in Altnagelvin and the other in Royal Belfast Children's Hospital. I showed them all the letters I had sent to relevant consultants and the senior managers in the Trust, about the mismanaged children. They wanted to take the letters, but I refused, explaining that the children's names on the documents constituted a breach of confidentiality. I told them that despite raising concerns I had little or no response from my colleagues. They had also spoken to Royal College of Paediatrics and Child Health (RCPCH).

After several months, the medical director spoke to me in the corridor and told me that he had initiated an investigation into the child deaths. My colleagues remained silent. I didn't receive any help or support from them. People were afraid to speak up and opted to close ranks as they were afraid of losing their jobs.

I had a second meeting with the TV team in Enniskillen at my home and had further discussions. They wanted me to speak on TV, but I declined. However, when the programme was shown on TV, I saw that I had been secretly filmed and depicted as a whistle-blower. I told the TV team that because of the unfriendly environment and blame and bullying culture I had decided to resign; known as a "constructive dismissal".

After a few months the programme was broadcast on local TV, but as I was working in England at the time, I asked one of my friends to record it and send the tape to me. One evening I was sitting in my flat when the tape arrived. I put it on and started watching. At the beginning the presenter was speaking to the mother of the girl who had been admitted to Erne hospital, Enniskillen with gastroenteritis and had unfortunately died. The mother spoke about her daughter's illness. Gastroenteritis is usually a self-limiting (will resolve on its own and/or no long-term consequences) mild disease and is corrected by oral - or in severe cases - intravenous fluid. She described the events of that night when the girl was admitted and commenced on IV fluid. Sometime during the night, she deteriorated and had convulsions. She was describing to the presenter that when this happened it was utter panic and chaos. Everybody in the ward was running around. The anaesthetist was called in and she was resuscitated, ventilated and transferred to the Royal Belfast hospital. From my perspective, the morning after this chaos when I came to the ward, I was told about the disaster that had happened overnight. One of the nurses who was involved in her resuscitation said, "they transferred the dead girl to Belfast to save their own skin".

The mother was so upset as I watched her on TV that she couldn't speak legibly about her daughter's death and started crying. I couldn't control my emotions and tears were flowing down my face. Nobody could imagine a mother's anger and anguish of this travesty; a totally avoidable death. I felt so sad and depressed that with all the medical care in the western world, a mother was grieving for her daughter's death which was preventable. The programme also mentioned the two other children who had died in similar circumstances in other hospitals. The TV team found it hard to speak to the doctors and the managers involved. They chased down the chief executive who would not talk to them. Eventually they waited for him in the hospital where he was having a meeting. When he came out, they managed to corner him but he remained tight-lipped.

The TV show became the trigger for a series of investigations, known as the "Hyponatraemia inquiry", announced in 2004, which investigated the suspect deaths of five children at the Royal Belfast Hospital. The O'Hara report was published in 2018, finding that four deaths were avoidable. It stated that the inquiry had been met with defensiveness and deceit, that information was withheld, evidence of a cover-up, poor care was deliberately concealed and a reluctance among clinicians to openly acknowledge failings[8].

I remember one evening I received a phone call from the editor of the *The Impartial Reporter*. We had a lengthy discussion about everything that happened with the mismanagement of children on the ward and he asked me if he could publish our chat in the newspaper. I had no objection.

---

[8] Available at http://www.ihrdni.org/Full-Report.pdf

60

NEWSPAPER CLIPPING FOLLOWING THE MISMANAGEMENT OF
CHILDREN IN ERNE HOSPITAL

Dr. Asghar's revelations come in the wake of a disturbing report which resulted in the new Health Minister, Mr. Shaun Woodward stepping in to protect patients in the Erne Hospital and the Tyrone County Hospital in Omagh, both managed by the Sperrin Lakeland Trust.

Mr Woodward said he was "appalled" at the findings of the report; which highlighted that risks to patients were being ignored.

The Trust's Chief Executive, Mr Hugh Mills, was forced to resign and the Trust is in crisis.

The report said: "We heard of a considerable number of examples of where adverse clinical incidents had occured, where staff had reported such incidents formally and informally, where they received little or no feedback, and where nothing had been done about the incident."

Dr. Asghar has given an interview to the Impartial Reporter, outlining in practical terms what is meant by "adverse clinical incidents".

One little girl had been given so much fluid that she developed pulmonary oedema and only survived after being transferred to Belfast. This condition sees a dangerous build-up of fluid in the lungs.

A young boy had suffered hyponatraemia (the condition from which Lucy Crawford died) and needed urgent treatment, which was not given. He was also transferred to Belfast and also survived. Despite Dr. Asghar writing to the Trust, nothing was done.

While giving examples of conditions, Dr. Asghar insists on keeping confidential details of patient identity to himself.

He also wrote to the Trust following the death of Lucy Crawford, highlighting his suspicions over her fluid management; yet the doctors involved in her treatment and the Sperrin Trust management continued to evade telling the Crawford family the truth. And it only emerged four years later at an inquest that Lucy had, in fact, died as a result of serious errors in the Erne.

The Impartial Reporter also understands that an inquest is pending on another child, who died in the Erne some time after Lucy. Dr. Asghar also raised concerns over her fluid management.

Alarmingly, these examples are only from one doctor over a short period and in one speciality.

The doctor said this week: "Nobody was taking the concerns that I was raising seriously. Either they did not realise the seriousness of the situation or they deliberately did not want to."

But Dr. Asghar insists: "There can be no more blame, culture and closing of ranks when something goes wrong.

"We are moving from a culture of secrecy to one of transparency; we are providing a service and we should be open to patients.

"It is time to treat patients with dignity and compassion, not as inhuman objects," said Dr. Asghar.

Dr. Mohammed Asghar

The doctor pointed out that hospitals conduct confidential inquiries every year on adverse incidents; for example patients who die within 24 hours of coming into hospital or patients who die under anaesthetic. He has taken part in such inquiries, but often finds discussion is not open.

"It is the culture of secrecy; if something has gone wrong, people are afraid of losing their jobs," he said.

He believes that Hugh Mills had to resign because "as Chief Executive he should have put the right systems in place so that mishaps and critical incidents do not happen."

The culture of closing ranks, however, has cost Dr. Asghar his job at the Erne hospital and he has moved away with his wife and family.

"I found it extremely stressful and difficult to convince my senior colleagues that there was something wrong and there needed to be improvements.

"Whistle blowing is always difficult. General Medical Council guidelines say that doctors and nursing staff should raise concerns, and I did that. But it is easier said than done," said Dr. Asghar, who believed that management often engaged in "paper flying around in paying lip service" in dealing with problems.

He has, however, praised the anaesthetists at the hospitals for raising their concerns over patient safety last year, directly with the Department of Health.

"They did the right thing," said Dr. Asghar. "Their concerns must have been serious."

There have been problems at the hospitals managed by the Trust for some time. Staff shortages, for example, continue to be a major problem, particularly at the children's ward at the Erne. There are also major issues in the area of social work.

Resources have been an issue, particularly following the uncertainty surrounding Trust's failure to press on with the implementation of the new hospital for the south-west at Enniskillen.

But the Trust's management method of dealing with things was to ignore the problems and try to continue providing services which were putting patients at risk.

Last autumn, the anaesthetists at the hospital became so frustrated with the situation that they contacted the Department of Health.

A steering group was set up last November, under the chairmanship of Mr Terence Lewis, a consultant surgeon in Plymouth.

It is this report that proved so damning of the Sperrin Lakeland Trust. Yet the Trust was preparing last week to brush even this report under the carpet.

It was allocated just 10 minutes at a com-

Hugh Mills

There can be no more blame culture and closing of ranks when something goes wrong. We are moving from a culture of secrecy to one of transparency; we are providing a service and we should be open to patients. It is time to treat patients with dignity and compassion, not as inhuman objects.

mittee meeting to be held at Coleshill in Enniskillen last Thursday morning. That is until one member of the steering group informed the Department of Health that she would go public on the seriousness of the report.

The report then went to the highest level, and when the new Health Minister read it, he was "appalled" and insisted on the Sperrin Lakeland Trust calling a full emergency board meeting. It was also made clear that this was a resignation issue, and the Chief Executive Hugh Mills was forced to quit.

That, however, is unlikely to be the end of the matter, so deep-rooted are the issues which go right to the top of the Department of Health.

• *Full reports on pages 6 and 7*

CONSTRUCTIVE DISMISSAL

While not as black and white as moving from east to west, living and working in England was still very different to Ireland. We had many good friends in Ireland and were well-settled there. I never truly wanted to move. I enjoyed the relaxed lifestyle in Ireland but the dysfunctional team, hostile atmosphere and the blame and bullying culture in the paediatric department in Erne hospital forced me to resign.

I started working in Canterbury hospital in East Kent. One day I called my sister in Pakistan and told her that we had moved to Canterbury, and being a Professor of English literature, her reaction was very positive. She said, "It's a beautiful place, you must go and watch The Canterbury Tales." I had read Chaucer's text but never had a chance to go to theatre. Canterbury was a beautiful place, an old, historic city with a magnificent cathedral, thriving with young people and daily tourists from across the Channel. A lively town with music playing in the town centre and plenty of junk food in the stalls.

The hospital in Canterbury was a lot busier and hectic than Enniskillen. This was a district general hospital with a children's ward, a day investigation unit and a very busy neonatal unit. The nursing staff were not very helpful. Most of them were consumed by their tasks and were very reserved. That cheeriness that I felt from my Irish colleagues was lacking. Everybody worked like a machine to finish their assigned task. Prior to the interview I had met a few consultant colleagues and one of them assured me that this was a very friendly team.

During my time there I learned neonatal procedures, high frequency ventilation and the community care of children discharged from hospital who needed long term care at home. I used to visit them at home with nurses. This was an integrated hospital and community care model which I found interesting.

After two years, when I left the hospital, the staff did arrange a leaving "do" for me with a card saying, "Good luck in Barrow".

On 1st of April 2005 I started working at Furness General Hospital, University Hospital of Morecambe Bay NHS Trust (UHMB), in Barrow-in-Furness.

Starting a new job is always exciting and you want to contribute positively in areas that need improvement. One meets new colleagues, sees a new working environment and makes new friends. It's always a new exciting experience. And that's how I felt, at least at the beginning. Unfortunately, my happiness was only short lived.

*

At the interview I was asked if I had any community experience. I had worked in the community while in Northern Ireland and in Canterbury, but it was not a large part of my job. I had visited schools and homes where children with long term disabilities needed care, had attended community meetings and held community clinics but my experience was still limited. The post I was applying for was newly created, a "generic paediatrician". A generic paediatrician's role was supposed to be looking after the children in community, as well as working in the hospital. It was a nice idea from the Royal College of Paediatrics which followed the journey of a child from the hospital to community. At the interview I was told I would be trained in community medicine and that I would learn on the job. I was promised that I would be supported to gain experience in community medicine. I accepted the role.

Learning on the job proved difficult. I was working alongside an experienced, fully trained community paediatrician. I tried to improve my knowledge in community medicine and attended several courses but quickly found that this was insufficient. A community paediatrician has to be trained like any other speciality such as cardiology, etc. The Trust and Primary Care Trust (PCT) as it was called at that time, were trying to fill up posts in Morecambe Bay, especially the newly created generic paediatrician post. The senior managers and clinical directors were keen to employ people to show their own efficiency. I realised that I had been lured into the job and that somebody like me, trained as a general paediatrician and in neonatology, should not have accepted a "community" job.

I tried my best but soon the staff and patients realised that I wasn't an expert in community paediatrics. The staff raised concerns about my community practice in clinics and the patients also started to ask that they would like to be seen by the other fully trained, experienced community paediatrician. Everybody kept comparing me to this other community paediatrician.

One day I received a letter from the medical director that the Trust would be investigating my clinical practice in community clinics to assess my competency. The same senior directors who were present at the interview and had assured me that I would "learn on the job" and "support me" had now turned around and initiated an investigation into my competency under MHPS (Maintaining High Professional Standards). In my entire professional career, I was never subjected to such an investigation. I had always considered myself as a hardworking, honest and dedicated doctor caring for patients to the best of my ability. The stress affected my family as well as myself. The strangest thing was that I was not suspended from my community work and I continued to hold community clinics. An independent external investigator was brought in who began sitting in on my clinical practice. He spoke to my colleagues, nursing staff and patients and sent patients records seen by me to an external consultant community paediatrician for further assessment.

I suffered an extremely stressful period in my life. Initially, I found it very difficult to reveal to my family that I was under investigation but in the end, I had to tell them. I would go to bed thinking about the investigation and wake up thinking about it. I would rise in middle of the night and start writing answers to the questions raised about my clinical practice. I had lost any sort of sleeping pattern. I would dream about the ongoing investigation; life had come to a standstill and was just revolving around my MHPS investigation.

Even though I kept working in acute paediatrics and neonatology my mind was occupied with the ongoing community investigation. I consulted literature and kept writing and justifying my clinical practice where some of the inexperienced community nursing staff had raised concerns that I had not treated or followed up patients properly. I later found out that the nursing staff's concerns were given more importance than my descriptions of managing patients. The Medical Protection Society (MPS) supported me during this investigation. It took more than two years to complete the community investigation.

In summary, the external investigator concluded:

"The creation of the novel post of generic consultant paediatrician should have been accompanied by more detailed preparation with tailored support being arranged for the successful candidates…"

"Dr […], Dr Asghar's clinical director when he was appointed, described his serious concerns about the difficult working environment into which Dr Asghar was appointed…"

"There is no evidence of misconduct by Dr Asghar. He is a committed clinician working in an at times hostile environment…"

*

Overall Discussion

Creation of the novel post of Generic Consultant Paediatrician should have been accompanied by more detailed preparation with tailored support being arranged for the successful candidates, Dr Asghar's and Dr ████████ Dr Asghar has included much evidence describing his acceptance of his development needs e.g. ADHD;

MA: We are talking about ADHD. It is not right that I refuse to see these children. I did say when I started working in 2005. I told Dr ████████████████████ that I don't have much experience in ADHD. I never said I refuse to see any suspected ADHD. That was six years ago. Over the past six years I have done so much work in ADHD, ██ agreed and was very supportive, and any courses relating to ADHD, autism, he agreed to. I must say he went out of his way to agree o these and was very supportive and I have improved a lot. Now I am treating and managing children with ADHD, even though it is a speciality area with complex behavioural problems. There are certain areas of ADHD which fall into the psychiatric domain.

If I have mismanaged any child with ADHD I would like to know. I have never refused, appendix 21

There is in the Terms of Reference gaps in my knowledge of ADHD. I made crystal clear to everyone I have little experience of ADHD. I have not seen children with ADHD and have little experience of it, but I did not refuse to see patients. I told them I didn't have much experience but was keen to learn. I have community related CPDs, and am able to provide evidence from the acute side of my CPD. appendix 22.

Additionally, standard support mechanisms for any consultant's post appear to have been absent e.g. appraisal, objective setting and job planning. Dr Asghar's first appraisal did not take place until November 2007, appendix 26, appraisal documentation 1.11.2007. The next took place in January 2011, appendix 27, Dr Asghar's appraisal documentation January 2011.

Dr ████ Dr Asghar's Clinical Director when he was appointed described his serious concerns about the ████████ working environment into which Dr Asghar was appointed. He said he would find it difficult to apportion blame, either to the individual practitioner or the system they were working in, appendix 10.

Conclusions and Recommendations

Dr ████████ concluded his tabular report by making several recommendations and drawing conclusions about Dr Asghar's practice and the system in which he was working in FGH. These are reproduced in full below as they carry the weight of clinical expertise and consequent validity.

The other requirement of the terms of reference is to if possible indicate whether these are issues of capability conduct or ill health as defined within MHPS.

There is no evidence of misconduct by Dr Asghar. He is a committed clinician working in an at times hostile environment. This is demonstrated in appendices 21, 22, 24, 25, 26, 27 and perhaps expressed most graphically in appendix 26, correspondence with ████████

There is no evidence of ill health contributing to the issues explored in this investigation which leads to the conclusion that the cause of the problems is Dr Asghar's capability to deliver the responsibilities of the post of Generic Consultant Paediatrician.

Dr ████████ conclusions and recommendations anticipate the possibility of Dr Asghar continuing to deliver community responsibilities or concentrating on General Hospital Paediatrics.

In 2005, when I started working with Morecambe Bay Trust, I soon noticed some inappropriate midwifery practices in the maternity unit. Senior midwives appeared to be in charge rather that the consultant obstetricians. Midwives would not allow or even call the obstetricians or paediatricians at times. Midwives would not allow the paediatricians to go into the labour room. If a baby needed immediate paediatric intervention or resuscitation, especially in the case of a preterm baby, the baby was brought out on the Resuscitaire[9] which was situated in a small room between two corridors with doors open on both sides. This inevitably caused babies to become hypothermic.

I raised my concerns in the senior consultant meetings which we used to have on weekly basis. I informed the clinical director about my concerns, but they were ignored, and no action was taken. I noted there were other concerns about the staffing level and particularly junior doctors without neonatal experience being left on their own to deal with deliveries. This left the junior doctors and babies in a very vulnerable position. A few junior doctors raised their concerns with consultants and informed their medical defence union. I myself wrote to the medical protection society and HCSA (Hospital Consultants and Specialists Association) about the patient safety issues.

The consultant rota was onerous with consultant paediatricians sometimes working alone over the weekend for up to 64-72 hours without a junior or middle grade doctor, covering

---

[9] A special bed for new-borns to facilitate thermoregulation and resuscitation, if necessary

the children ward, special care baby unit, labour ward, caesarean sections in theatre and also A&E. The senior managers had realised this dangerous and unsafe situation and they asked all the consultant paediatricians to sign a declaration that they were willing to work in this way.

Hospital Consultants & Specialists Association

Number One, Kingsclere Road, Overton, Basingstoke, Hampshire, RG25 3JA
Tel: 01256 771777   Fax: 01256 770999
e-mail: cmspcd@hcsa.com   www.hcsa.com

Our Ref: SFBC2445/SJW   August 7th 2009

Dr. M. Asghar, MRCPI MRCPCH
Consultant Pædiatrician
Furness General Hospital
Dalton Lane
BARROWE IN FURNESS
LA14 4LF

Dear Dr. Asghar,

Thank you for your letter with enclosures about paediatric services. I have read the papers in some detail, leaving me to conclude that there are many difficult and complex issues that need to be resolved. Clearly the inadequate number of Consultants and junior medical staff has put great pressure on the services you seek to provide. I agree with the Medical Protection Society that where service levels pose a risk to patient safety these must be brought to the Trust's attention. In doing so you have in part, discharged your duties as a medical practitioner.

I say "in part" because I also believe that whereas Consultants may find themselves at the wrong end of the problem, they should also be part of the solution by working together and with Trust management to secure improvements. Reading between the lines it seems to be that the failure to appoint Consultants, retain junior staff and implement a model of Consultants residency has contributed to an air of despondency – and from that a "blame culture" appears to have emerged. These pressures will not disappear overnight but will be exacerbated unless there is effective team working amongst the key players.

I can therefore well understand, and from experience am not at all surprised by, the tensions that exist. The trick is to use perceptions positively, as an aid firstly to get agreement on what the problem is. That is easier said than done because clearly people will have their own perceptions of the problem – some may even refuse to acknowledge that a problem exists.

Against this context the advice I would offer is that "the team" however defined must somehow come to consensus agreement not only about the problem(s) but work together and positively towards resolution.

Continued/......

REPLY TO MY RAISED CONCERNS

MEDICAL PROTECTION SOCIETY
Granary Wharf House, Leeds LS11 5PY, UK
DX 12089 Leeds 1
Telephone 0845 605 4000
International code +44 113 243 6436
Facsimile +44 (0) 113 241 0500

www.mps.org.uk

Personal and Confidential
Dr M Asghar
Consultant Paediatrician
Furness General Hospital
Barrow in Furness
Cumbria
LA14 4LF

Please quote our reference when contacting MPS

17 March 2008

Dear Dr Asghar

Thank you very much for your recent correspondence in this matter.

Having looked at the material you have forwarded to me I can see that your main concerns effectively revolve around the issue of resources and in particular the resources available to back up the junior staff whilst on call.

As has already been done in the past, I think the only sensible way forward here is for you to draw your concerns to the Trust management in writing. In doing so you would need to point out that firstly you were complying with the requirements of your contract but that secondly nevertheless (for the reasons that you have so clearly explained to me) have concerns because of the potential risk to patients. You could then go on to propose that there should be a meeting with Trust management to try and formulate an action plan to resolve the outstanding issues.

As you rightly point out at the end of your letter, if a patient suffered avoidable harm as a result of a lack of or inadequacy of resources, it would be the Trust as a body that would be responsible. A doctor in these circumstances discharges his responsibility by assuring that the concerns are clearly raised with management in writing.

I do hope that this advice helps you to move the matter forward. If there are any further issues that you would like me to expand on or clarify please do not hesitate to let me know.

Yours sincerely

Head of Medical Services Leeds

Secretary
Direct Telephone   0113 241 0369
Direct Facsimile   0113 241 0501
Email   medical.leeds@mps.org.uk

The Medical Protection Society Limited

1 of 1

One day I received a phone call from the clinical director that the CQC (Care Quality Commission) were visiting the hospital and he told me not to talk to them. I had never heard of the CQC before, so I asked him to explain. He gave me a brief summary of their role and advised me that if they asked any questions, I should not discuss anything with them. Instead, I should direct them to the communication team of the Trust. I wondered if this was a cover-up strategy by the Trust managers.

The CQC inspected all the departments in all three Hospitals of Morecambe Bay Trust and the paediatric and maternity units in Furness General Hospital where I worked. They branded the maternity unit in FGH as, "not fit for purpose". An investigation was initiated by the CQC. The medical records of mothers and babies who had died over the past several years were passed on to the CQC and Cumbria Constabulary.

Amidst this investigation, an anonymous report was sent to the General Medical Council about me - I suspect by a middle manager in the Trust. They (incorrectly) accused me of not treating a new-born baby properly at the time of birth. The mother was GBS (Group B Streptococcus positive) during pregnancy. The baby was discharged from maternity ward as he was well. Later, at the age of four weeks, the baby became unwell and was admitted to the paediatric ward, and unfortunately died of late onset GBS meningitis. I was not working when this baby was born, nor was I on-call. I reiterate, I never saw the baby at the time of his birth.

While the investigation into my community clinics was ongoing, a second investigation was opened against me. I received a letter from the GMC that I would be investigated with regards to my clinical practice. Shock is a very small word to describe what was happening to me. Looking back, I'm not sure how I survived the stress. I repeatedly told the clinical director, senior managers and nursing staff that I was not involved in looking after the newborn baby at the time of birth, but nobody would listen to me. Finally, a locum senior nurse gave me copy of an RCA (Root Cause Analysis) about the baby which was performed four months after the baby had died. This was done without my knowledge and without involving me. It concluded that, "…this baby was managed appropriately in accordance with the guidelines".

University Hospitals **NHS**
of Morecambe Bay
NHS Foundation Trust

Incident Details

Incident Date	Time	PSI	Riddor	SUI	Risk Rating	Reference	Web Ref	Form No
13/02/2011	21:45			✓	Moderate (Orange)			

Subjects Of Incident

Staff/Person/Other   Role   ID1

       Patient

Incident Details

Organisation	University Hospitals Of Morecambe Bay NHS		Directorate	Women And Children's
Site	Furness General Hospital		Specialty	Obstetrics
Site Type	General Hospital		Location	
Department	Maternity Unit FGH		Location Detail	
Division			Referred To	Ward Doctor

Cause Group	Maternity		Initial Severity	Major
Cause 1	Neonatal Death		Initial Likelih'd	Rare
Cause 2			Initial R Rating	Moderate (Orange)
Incident Type	Clinical Incident		Severity	Major
Entered By			Likelihood	Rare
Completed By			Risk Rating	Moderate (Orange)
Reported	07/03/2011 - 18:23		Actual Impact	5 Catastrophic
Con. Factors				

Incident Description

Baby 3 weeks and 5 days of age re-admitted to children's ward in a collapsed state. Stabilised and transferred to Royal Manchester Childrens ward the next morning. Died the same day (14/2/11).

Additional Details Supplied By Reporter

07/03/2011 ; 18:23

Case to be followed up via maternity incident process

Lessons Learnt

24/09/2012 12:50

Comment from ▇▇▇▇▇▇
we have reviewed the maternal records to review care of the mother - report not yet finished. The mother was identified as Group B Streptococcus (GBS) ve and treated accordingly with intrapartum IV antibiotics - as per Guidance
I presume paediatrics would do the review of the baby??
I have not had written confirmation but have been told that the cause of death was 'late onset GBS'
It will be formally discussed at the next CIR meeting

Update from ▇▇▇▇▇▇ 28.4.11: I discussed this with both ▇▇▇▇▇▇
The cause of death was late onset GBS
This baby was managed appropriately in accordance with the guidelines as-
Mother did only have one risk factor. (Baby would be given antibiotics if mother had two risk factors.)
Baby was well

Update from ▇▇▇▇ 28.4.11: I was not directly involved in this

As far as aware baby did not trigger 2 risk factors on the flowchart and did not get antibiotics following delivery. Late onset GBS would not present with symptoms in the immediate period following delivery

I think ▇▇▇▇▇▇ reviewed the history shortly after the baby end decided that the flowchart had been appropriately followed and no changes were required

16/10/2013

Page 1

CONFIRMING MY APPROPRIATE HANDLING OF A CASE I WASN'T
DIRECTLY INVOLVED IN

University Hospitals **NHS**
of Morecambe Bay
NHS Foundation Trust

Incident Details

Internationally, surveillance and treatment in the neonatal period for GBS has decreased cases by 80 percent but not irradicated it completely. We cannot guarantee that the guideline is 100 effective at preventing invasive disease for this reason.

Quality & Governance Team Comments

27/10/2011 : 10:19

08.02.10 - Incident submitted with incorrect department (medical records) in error. Changed to Maternity and appropriate staff notified - IR Dept.
27.10.11 - Request from FACS Governance lead for copy of incident report, sent as requested via email.

Outcome Details

Outcome Type   No Further Action Required

Regardless, the GMC team came down to FGH and investigated my clinical practice. They collected patient records, met some of my consultant and nursing colleagues and asked them about my clinical practice, behaviour and general conduct. When they interviewed me, I was completely transparent and gave them as much information as I could. I had to undergo a clinical test including an MCQ (multiple choice question) paper and clinical scenarios. The assessors report was submitted to the Medical Director on 21st of March 2014. It concluded that, "the practitioner's professional performance has not been deficient, and practitioner is fit to practice generally."

The GMC team also noted the following and reported, "…throughout the Peer Review and Tests of Competence the team gathered contextual information about Dr Asghar and his practice:

- Problems in the working environment.
- Resident first on-call duties.
- Leadership and fairness do not exist. Clinical Director is reluctant to do job plans and avoid issues.
- Multitude of problems, mainly staffing and leadership issues and personal relationships and relationships between Royal Lancaster Infirmary and FGH.
- No proper way of raising concerns, governance issues which are not handled appropriately.

- PSIs (patient safety incidents) were not addressed at the time and the proper procedures were not carried out.

- Secretarial support always deficient.

- Safety of service issues.

- Despite raising his concerns, strong feelings, his concerns were not listened to. There is a large gulf between Consultants and managers.

I asked the clinical and medical director who had written the incorrect report and sent it to the GMC. I received no answer. I asked the newly appointed medical director the same question. He refused to answer. I asked the Medical Protection Society to formally write to him and ask the same question. MPS wrote to him. He chose not to respond.

Nobody was ever held accountable. My suspension lasted two years. After this, I received a single letter of apology from the former medical director.

The Kirkup report [10] was published in early 2015. It highlighted severe problems in the maternity department in FGH, between 2004-2013, and published their recommendations. The report described a seriously dysfunctional maternity unit, substandard clinical competence, poor working relationships including a strong group mentality/tribalism among midwives,

---

[10] Available at
https://assets.publishing.service.gov.uk/government/uploads/system/uploads/attachment_data/file/408480/47487_MBI_Accessible_v0.1.pdf

failures of risk assessment and care planning, deficient responses to adverse incidents and repeated failures to investigate thoroughly. The report found twenty instances of major failures at FGH, including three maternal deaths, and sixteen baby deaths.

University Hospitals **NHS**
of Morecambe Bay
NHS Foundation Trust

Our Ref: ▮

<Sent Via Email>

Dr Muhammad Aaghar
Consultant Paediatrician
FGH

Trust Headquarters
Westmorland General Hospital
Burton Road
Kendal
LA9 7RG

Tel: 01539 716966
Fax: 01539 795313
Web: www.uhmb.nhs.uk

08 September 2014

Dear Muhammad,

Re: Meeting on Tuesday 2ⁿᵈ September 2014, WGH.

Thank you for meeting with myself and ▮ on Tuesday. You had raised concerns about the documentation that had been passed to the GMC as part of the ongoing police enquiry into maternity services at FGH in 2012. It was clear to both ▮ and I that no aspect of your management of patient ▮ (the patient referred to in the documentation forwarded to the GMC by Cumbria Constabulary) indicated any performance or practice concerns on your part.

There was a summary (letter) contained within the documentation with no indication as to who had compiled it, that inferred that you had been involved in the care of the baby at birth and soon afterwards, and made assertions about the baby being lethargic and a poor feeder at that time. However, it was clear from the contemporaneous records, that after birth the baby had not had documented feeding difficulties and was not lethargic as suggested in this summary (letter).

It was also clear from the notes and other documentation that in the period between the baby's birth on 18.01.2011 and post natal discharge on 20.01.11, you had not been involved in the care of that baby. There is no criticism about your subsequent management of the baby, when he was re-admitted as an emergency on 12.02.2011.

At the present time we do not know who compiled the summary letter, but nonetheless apologise unreservedly on behalf of the Trust for any distress caused as a consequence, of it being forwarded to the GMC. I am currently unaware of the sequence of events leading to the documentation being passed to the GMC by Cumbria Constabulary. The GMC subsequently requested documentation from myself which comprised the incident reports that have been shared with you and the related extracts from the patient's clinical notes, but not that related to ▮

We will endeavour to see if it is possible to identify at this interval by whom that summary (letter) was compiled.

Trust Headquarters
Westmorland General Hospital
Burton Road
Kendal
LA9 7RG
Tel: 01539 732288

INTERIM CHAIR: JOHN HUTTON
CHIEF EXECUTIVE: JACKIE DANIEL

CONFIRMATION OF MY FITNESS TO PRACTICE

As a consequence of the GMC enquiry and concerns that we had raised internally in relation to a large number of critical incident reports, you have undergone a GMC assessment. Subsequent to that assessment the team concluded that your performance was not deficient and that you are fit to practise generally. We fully accept the GMC findings and the recommendations that you be offered a phased and supported return to clinical practice. The investigation commenced by the GMC has been closed and so has that commenced by the Trust.

Yours sincerely

Medical Director

Copy To: ▮▮▮▮▮▮ Clinical Director Women & Children's Services.

EAST AND WEST

I still can't believe all this happened in a rich, developed country with plenty of resources, highly specialised modern hospitals, extensive primary care and with a National Health Service considered to be one of the best in the world. I have worked in developing countries with limited resources and I have seen disasters happening but did not expect such disasters to occur here.

I have realised that there is no doubt about the commitment and dedication from the majority of frontline staff. So, what goes wrong?

*

When I started working as a doctor after qualifying in Pakistan, there was no requirement to be a member of a medical defence union. In fact, none existed in Pakistan at that time. We only had to be registered with PMC (Pakistan Medical Council). We worked hard, day and night, with some departments in the hospitals looking after patients with a skeleton crew.

I was working in a tertiary neurosurgical unit as a junior house surgeon in Pakistan. We were a friendly team. The nursing staff would do night duties on a monthly basis i.e. a nurse used to be on night duty for one month continuously with some nights off. They used to call the last night of their duty at the end of the month "Golden Night". On Golden Night, they would cook and bring food to the ward and we would all eat together when the ward was a bit quieter after midnight. While we were eating a patient's relative walked into our office and said, "You are amazing. I can't believe that doctors and nurses work so hard. I can't believe you are having your evening meal at 2 AM". He was absolutely right as irregular meals, or sometimes no meals, were a norm.

During our education in the medical college the emphasis was on acquiring knowledge. The professors and other clinical teachers did their best to teach us. Now I realise there was something lacking in our curriculum; how to communicate with colleagues, patients, patients' relatives, how to listen, how to explain and how to treat patients with dignity. Empathy was not part of the curriculum.

As a 3rd year medical student I was doing my training in A&E. A child was brought in with a very high temperature and headache. The parents were obviously very distressed. The casualty medical officer examined the child and wrote down the treatment not explaining or even talking to the parents. The father came over to the medical officer and asked him what was wrong with his son. Instead of explaining, he became angry and said, "How can I explain to you? He has meningitis. Do you understand what meningitis is? I have written the treatment and he is getting it". The parents were obviously not very educated, and they quietly went and sat down in a corner.

There was no emphasis on teaching and learning communication skills. The people knew that their colleague had made a mistake or missed something, but they preferred to stay quiet; ignorance was a normal way of life. Respect for patients, listening to them, empathy, treating them with dignity, explaining and involving them in the decision-making process and communication skills never existed. I saw doctors getting angry with patients and their relatives and frustrated relatives verbally abusing the doctors. I remember one colleague working in Libya was beaten by the patient's relatives. He decided to become a radiologist just to remain away from the frontline.

If there were mistakes made by the doctors there was no system in place to learn lessons from their errors. There was no accountability. This was considered normal clinical practice.

*

Working in the west has its own set of problems. I came to Ireland and met a few friends from Pakistan who were also there to obtain higher training in different specialities. Some of them were my colleagues in the same college where I had qualified. One of my friends who was training to be a surgeon gave me some tips. He had been in Ireland a little longer than me. Some of the things he said included:

- Always try to protect yourself and watch your back.

- If you make a mistake nobody is going to help you here. They will drop you like a hot potato, so be a member of a medical defence union and always take advice from them.

- Document everything. Involve everybody. Don't work alone. Try your best to treat and manage the patients to be best of your ability but involve your seniors. Write clinical discussions down because if it's not in writing it didn't happen.

- Don't fight with the managers as they have power. Keep quiet even if something goes wrong. That's how it works here.

This was very useful and practical advice. But it also raised some concerns in my mind. If I saw something wrong happening or a patient's welfare or treatment being compromised or mistakes being covered-up how I could remain silent? I had worked very hard to pass the PLAB (Professional and Linguistic Board) and read through all GMC documents including good medical practice, which stated:

- Make the care of your patient your first concern.
- Take prompt action if you think patient safety, dignity and comfort is being compromised.

I must say that the NHS in the UK is one of the best health care systems in the world but there are still some flaws. The most striking feature I noticed was a constant, ongoing and non-resolving conflict between senior managers/directors and the frontline staff including senior consultants, junior doctors and the nursing staff. The priorities for the two groups were completely different even though both claimed to act in the best interest of the patient. Apparently, the managers' priority was to balance the books; they were more concerned about percentages and statistics while the frontline staff were more concerned about low staffing level resulting in unsafe onerous rotas and extra shifts for the remaining staff. As one of the consultants said, "You have to dance with whatever type of music the managers are playing".

As a junior doctor in Ireland I witnessed a strike by the non-consultant hospital doctors organised by the doctor's union over a dispute about long working hours. Similarly, there was another occasion when the frontline staff in Northern Ireland demonstrated against the closure of a hospital. They came out with placards saying, "You save money, we save lives".

When I started working in Ireland, I called one of my friends who was working in America to ask about his experiences there. He told me that in America when a patient comes out of the hospital, the medico-legal insurance companies start chasing them to see if they have any complaint about the hospital, "Are you happy with your treatment? Did anything go wrong? If so, we can sue the hospital and get you financial compensation."

The system in the western world is quasi-medico-legal and finance driven. It is absolutely necessary to be a member of a medical defence union. While working in an eastern country, you just jump in and try your best to help the patients. Working in a western country you still do the same but there is another aspect to it as well. Medics and paramedics tend to "cover" themselves just in case there is a mishap. People are scared about anything going wrong, anything missed or complaints from the patients, fearing an investigation.

I remember the first time a patient complained about me. A senior manager came over and asked me to respond to the complaint by submitting a written report. I felt and really believed that I had been a kind, attentive and hardworking doctor looking after patients very well and to the best of my ability. How could it have happened to me?

Patients were encouraged to complain if they were not happy about the care they had received. Patient feedback was encouraged. This was a good system to improve patient safety, care quality and to catch mistakes, but this was also associated with a lot of stress for the staff. Sometimes the patient safety incidences were not managed properly; typically, the doctor was not involved and the whole exercise appeared to be a secret affair.

Once a stressed junior doctor came to me and told me about a PSI (patient safety incidence) which a nurse had reported. He was in tears and needed emotional support. There had been incidences of young junior doctors committing suicide because of work-related stress. I still remember a German junior doctor who committed suicide by injecting herself with anaesthetic drugs. She had been working in the anaesthetic department and was probably familiar with the necessary medication.

Loneliness is a huge problem in western culture. In eastern culture, there may be friends and relatives to support during difficult times because of a traditional close-knit family culture. This is lacking in the west. However, there are many supportive organisations which can be contacted in difficult times, e.g. Samaritans. This concept may be foreign to foreigners, and hence many overseas doctors living in a western country tend to gravitate towards their own ethnic minorities.

I had moved from an eastern country to the west and wanted to learn and serve the patients to the best of my ability, but I hadn't prepared myself for the mental stresses I would encounter. In your professional life one has to find some sort of work-life balance. I have come to the conclusion that if you are not happy in any situation, just leave.

*

A blame and bullying culture is rampant in the NHS. People are afraid of losing their job and if something goes wrong, they either keep quiet or tend to blame somebody else. It's all about saving your own job from top to bottom. A lot of people don't care about the imperfect system and make no effort to improve the service. Their thinking is that it's "not their headache". Particularly, I have seen first-hand, that overseas doctors can have a tendency to work mainly for monetary gains and return home after obtaining higher degrees or when they finish their training. Their attitude is, "This is not our country. Why should we bother?" Others may be content to live with the organisational failures and try to use the system for their own financial gains and advantage as much as possible.

System failures can occur in any organisation; a Swiss cheese model[11] will not prevent all losses. From my experience with the NHS, there is still a tendency to blame the individuals rather than trying to find out if there is anything wrong with the system.

There are whistle-blower policies in every Trust in the NHS, but they are hardly implemented. These are kept on the shelves and are good for decorative purposes, to pay lip-service to the CQC.

When something goes wrong the senior managers tend to scapegoat the staff to be perceived as if they are fixing the system.

---

[11] The Swiss cheese model likens human systems to multiple layers of "Swiss cheese", with holes of varying size and position. Each layer is a form of defence against a possible accident. Theoretically, most risks are mitigated since a direct line of sight or trajectory is unlikely from the first layer to the last.

In fact, *they* are the cause of the problem and organisational failure. The higher up you are on the managerial hierarchy, the less likely you are to lose your job, and the stronger the position you have, the easier it becomes to assassinate someone's career. If you join them, becoming part of the unchanging, flawed system, you can be praised and told you are a hero. The real heroes are actually those who stand up against the current, who stand up for patient safety and save lives.

EPILOGUE

Once my friend told me:

"You have worked in the NHS for 25 years but have learnt nothing. This is the NHS. Put your head down, do your job, take your money and go home. Staffing levels, training and retaining, quality assurance, driving up standards, waiting list initiatives, empowering patients, budgetary constraints and targets are all managerial jargon. Leave it to them. Don't fight with the managers. Don't be a whistle-blower. You are only inviting trouble for yourself and the wrath of the senior managers and directors".

In fact, a lot of doctors have a similar attitude. Once I was at a BAPIO (British Association of Physicians of Indian Origin) conference. I met a consultant physician who had been a whistle-blower at an NHS Trust. He delivered an eloquent speech at the conference describing how he had suffered at the hands of the senior managers and the medical director of the Trust. He had decided to stand up and speak out for the patients who were suffering. There was a legal battle and he had suffered enormous stress, mental anguish and health problems. At the end of the speech he received a standing ovation from the audience. After the conference I asked him, "Would you advise any doctor to be a whistle-blower?" He vehemently opposed it and said, "No, don't do it".

As a doctor I have never differentiated amongst people on the basis of their country of origin, their religious beliefs, colour or creed; these are just arbitrary lines drawn on Earth. I have never expected any reward or even thanks from the patients. I have tried my best to treat my patients to the best of my ability with care and compassion.

I have learnt that just like employers try to choose the best employees from the candidate pool, similarly you have to choose the best employer very wisely. I have said it before and I will say it again: even if you are an honest and hard-working person devoted to your profession, it does not mean that life is going to be easy for you. You need to be clever to steer the ship of your career through rough waters and not let toxic managerial waves capsize your boat.

At the end of my professional career the only satisfaction I have is that I had a chance to serve people and I have been able to treat thousands of patients and help alleviate their suffering. I believe that if you spread happiness it will come back to you. If I have been able to serve humanity, contributed towards the wellbeing of people and brought some happiness to their lives, then I have done my job.

APPENDIX

The following is further evidence confirming my fitness to practice following the investigation in Furness General Hospital. Additionally, I have added numerous newspaper clippings describing the events around the hyponatremia deaths in Northern Ireland.

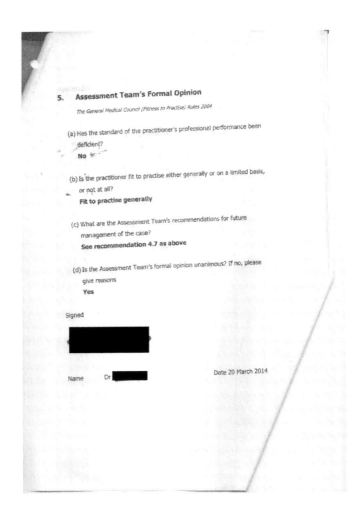

5. Assessment Team's Formal Opinion

The General Medical Council (Fitness to Practise) Rules 2004

(a) Has the standard of the practitioner's professional performance been deficient?

No

(b) Is the practitioner fit to practise either generally or on a limited basis, or not at all?

Fit to practise generally

(c) What are the Assessment Team's recommendations for future management of the case?

See recommendation 4.7 as above

(d) Is the Assessment Team's formal opinion unanimous? If no, please give reasons

Yes

Signed

Name   Dr

Date 20 March 2014

THE FOLLOWING ARE DOCUMENTS CONFIRMING MY COMPETENCY TO PRACTICE, AS WELL AS REVIEWING THE CONCERNS I HAVE RAISED ABOUT FURNESS GENERAL HOSPITAL

3.10 CONTEXT

3.10.1   Throughout the Peer Review and Tests of Competence the
Team gathered contextual information about Dr Asghar and his
practice. This assisted the Team in having a wider
understanding of the Trust within which he was working, and
staffing issues within that Trust, which, in the view of the Team
could have had a considerable bearing on the doctor's overall
performance historically. For this reason the Team judged it
important to include this information in the body of the Report
rather than as an appendix to the Report. Relevant entries
under the heading of Context are as described below:

3.10.2   TPI18-270 His community practices have impacted on his acute
practice – he was unhappy and felt unsupported. Given hard
cases – unable to cope with. After Resident On-Call System felt
he is *"shattered"*. Colleagues concerned about him. Consultant
has to deal unsupported with a range of demands. Following
him stopping community work he became more relaxed and had
more time for his acute work. Plenty of common sense at this
stage of his career. Those 2 pressures have impacted and
affected him.

3.10.3   TPI11-40 (Problems in the working environment). Resident First
On-Call Duties, lack of secretarial support. The on-call
frequency was onerous. The onerous On-Call may have
impacted on his ability to undertake community work. He was
also not trained to do community work.

TPI18-40 A Consultant Resident in Hospital on your own
dealing with (a) variety of issues; (b) lack of secretarial support;
(c) on-call system – on-call frequently – on-call impacted upon

abilities; (d) appointment as a Generic Consultant but then expected to do community work for which he is not trained.

3.10.4   TPI3-270 During the last few weeks, months, he was more forgetful and was not as clear and would ask things several times. He would ask for things to be repeated and sometimes he got things wrong when he checked back information to her. There was a lot of stress around the Organisation as a whole at the time. Not sure if he was under personal stress or it was generally a stressful atmosphere.

3.10.5   TPI2-40 (Working environment problems). There were not many Junior Doctors then or now – no middle grade staff – may have been 2 then.

3.10.6   TPI8-40 Leadership and fairness does not exist. Clinical Director reluctant to do Job Plans and avoid issues. Issues like PSI not handled or addressed soon after the procedure or in a timely fashion.

3.10.7   TPI5-40 Yes a multitude of problems, mainly staffing and leadership issues and personal relationships and relationships between Royal Lancaster Infirmary and FGH (working environment issues).

3.10.8   TPI17-41 The Mitchell Report – to look at Children's Services across both sides and the Community Services. Findings not liked – Report was rubbished. Put on a shelf. Nothing happened. There is no equality of pay, there is friction. No Job Plans since 2006. 20 PSI s not dealt with at the time when they occurred.

3.10.9   TPI5-50 A situation of learned helplessness arose – similar
          issues were raised verbally and in writing, e.g. in e-mails to
          make Managers aware of his concerns and of other Consultants
          from Senior's meeting with Managers, Senior Nurse,
          Consultants, CAHMS. On the agenda since 2005 when he came.
          No proper way of raising concerns, governance issues which are
          not handled appropriately. Similar issues in 2001 and in Andy
          Mitchell's Report in around 2008 looking at community issues as
          well as Hospital ones – children's issues across both main sites,
          also CAHMS Services and the interactions between Acute and
          Community Services. Nothing happened. An issue about poor
          leadership. No fairness, e.g. parity of pay. Dr Asghar. did not
          have a Job Plan from 2006 for 5 years. The 20 PSI s were not
          addressed at the time and the proper procedures were not
          carried out – mainly system issues, e.g. Ambulance Service.

3.10.10   TPI7-270 Have found him to be a quiet, pleasant, professional
          gentleman. Coming into work daily to see his colleagues in a
          work setting has been courageous (for a Doctor suspended from
          clinical duties). She has a lot of respect for him. The whole
          situation (is restricted to non-clinical duties) has dragged on for
          a long time which on reflection could have been avoided. She
          was very surprised to find from her own personal experience in
          other Trusts how long this has taken in Morecambe Bay – a year
          later and still going on.

3.10.11   FI1-100 Secretarial support always deficient. Consultant
          numbers increased, Secretary numbers reduced to 4 from 5. All
          Consultants felt the same that secretarial support was
          inadequate. The room allocated as On-Call Room kept
          changing. Sometimes he was put in the Parents Room or slept
          on SCBU. The rooms had telephones unless they were put in

the doctors' residences when rooms 9,10 and 11 were in use. There was no designated room at that time, so he never knew where he was going to be staying.

3.10.12   FI1-110 (Clarifying the nature of his appointment in 2005) It was called a Generic Paediatrician Consultant Post. His expectation was that he would do a small amount of community work, but mainly generic paediatric work in an outpatients, etc. He was expecting to see ordinary cases in community and not complex cases as he was not trained in Autism or ADHD work.

3.10.13   FI3-130 There were patient safety incidents (PSIs) from May 2010 to May 2012. The *"community"* investigation was ongoing. Two of the PSI reports were judged by the MD as serious. The remainder were judged to be of low severity.

3.10.14   FI1-150 He (Dr Asghar) drew our attention to inaccuracies in the GMC background summary to the case which we had seen and he supplied us with documentation to support that. He apologised for getting upset about this but it does upset him when lies continued to be put in print that he thought would colour our view about him. The Team Leader reiterated that our task was to look at his performance and not the complaints which had been made about him.

This refers to the baby who died of GBS meningitis

3.10.15   FI1-20 (In connection with his training experiences). Most of the training was in the Republic of Ireland. Worked as Registrar Junior Doctor in Ireland 1981 onwards; for years there were no structure training at that time. He applied for different posts after completing training. He applied to be on the Specialist Register in Ireland and was accepted. Submitted evidence to the GMC and did it by the Article 14 route.

3.10.16   FI1-30 He did the MRCPI in 1993. Passed Part 1 of the MRCPCH at the same time. When he was trying to get on the Specialist Register had to do Part 1 again for MRCPCH and completed it in 2003 by examination.

3.10.17   FI1-40 In July, 2012 activities restricted. Since then was told he was not suspended. Medical Director said he could do RCA – has had training for this. He has been Lead in some of them – 5-6 in total. Has continued teaching activities since he stepped down being College Tutor in 2011 which he did for 3 years. He has carried on doing Audits. He has been allocated 4 Audits: ADHD, Chronic Fatigue Syndrome, Depression in Children, Behavioural Disorders in Children. Serious Case Review as well. Chaired 2 Guideline Groups. Has also been involved in complaints as well. Looking at whether they are following the Guidelines.

3.10.18   FI1-50 (Clarifying his timetable). Timetable on Page 21 referred to his work from 2005 onwards. When he stopped doing community clinics by arrangement with the Clinical Director he could do Acute OP Clinics instead. There were initially 4 Consultants on the rota in 2005, now up to 10 Consultants.

3.10.19   FI1-51 He was asked about how many PA's he was doing and asked about clinical work. Major discrepancies between Consultants. He had a temporary PA contract 2 others had 12 PA's. He raised it with Clinical Director but it never materialised. He thought he was doing far more – he completed a workload diary – came out at 12.3 PA's. First Job Plan took place in 2010 after he had been in post for 5 years despite requesting he should have one.

3.10.20 FI1-60 Started substantive post January, 2006 (Locum for months before). In HOT week no routine work. Emergencies, 4 on-call for Labour Ward and Sections, etc., 9.00 a.m. to 5.00 p.m. From 2006 to February, 2009 did this 1:4 – 9.00 a.m. to 5.00 p.m. but could be doing nights as well. It was a big governance issue. Consultants stayed at home whilst on-call relatively unskilled staff were on the grounds in wards and theatres, etc. Junior Doctors and GP Trainees. (He provided supporting evidence from 2006 in a document from Junior Doctors). In February, 2009 changed a Resident On-Call for Consultants. Between February, 2006 and February, 2009 could sometimes do 7 nights On-Call as well as being HOT week Consultant. At that stage there were middle grade doctors. 2010 and 2011 no middle grades at all – 2-3 junior doctors only.

3.10.21 FI1-70 Shift System came in from July, 2012 to replace the Resident On-call Rota when they were staying in Hospital but there was an SHO there too. Before the Shift System started in 2011 could be doing 64 hour weekends (he gave us documentation to support this). He felt in 2011 to 2012 he was the Consultant and Junior Doctor doing those long hours – this was when the *"20 incidents"* happened. He gave us an OH Report to support that assertion.

3.10.22 FI1-80 (Middle Grade cover). Five Staff Grade Posts were advertised but no-one applied. There were Visa problems country-wide to account for this.

3.10.23   F11-90 There has been a gradual increase from 2011
from 4 to current level of 10 Consultants. After July 2012
when the Shift System was in place, minimum number of
Consultants needed to be 10. He felt junior doctor levels
were not adequate in 2011/2012. They were still
working all weekend alone without Juniors.

3.10.24   SI1-30 We had a meeting with other colleagues and
AMD brought to their attention he was doing over 14 PA's
paid for 10 PA's – response from AMD was diary is dead
now (following a diary keeping and monitoring exercise).
Ernst and Young had been brought in to steer this
process through and he felt all the money paid out to
them was down the drain. No Job Plan came out of this
expense. First Job Plan was in 2010.

3.10.25   SI1-31 Safety of Service issues. Despite raising his
concerns, strong feeling, his concerns were not listened
to. Big gulf between Consultants and Managers.
Commented on by Sir ███████ when he was
brought in early 2012. He was here for 12 months
approximately. There was a change in top management
of the Team. New people brought in to address safety of
Maternity Services and poor Midwifery practices, babies
dying, etc. Striving to improve the safety of services. In
Paediatrics. Number of Consultants increased. Resident
On-call introduced. EWT brought in. In summary there
have been improvements in the Service.

3.10.26   ST2-20 Furness information from site tour. Furness
General Hospital is a small isolated Unit with a child
catchment population of approximately 20,000 children.

There are approximately 1,300 live births per annum. There is 24 hour Consultant residential cover with minimal Junior medical Staff cover during the day but not at night. There is no Community Paediatric presence on site.

3.10.27   ST2-30 In 2012 the Specialist Baby Care Unit (SCBU) was remote from the Maternity Unit. This has now been addressed and the SCBU has been relocated to a position within the Maternity Unit.

3.10.28   TPI2-270 I would be happy for him to look after my little boy, he listens to me. He was interested and caring about her son (not his patient) and enquired after him. I have not had any issues with him.

No resignations, no proper answers, and after four LONG years...

Trust: we killed Lucy

The Chief Executive of the organisation which manages the Erne Hospital says his Health Trust now accepts responsibility for the death of 17-month-old Lucy Crawford.

It has taken four years, but effectively he is admitting that bungling by the Enniskillen hospital killed the baby by pumping far too much of the wrong fluid into the little girl. Lucy was admitted suffering from gastroenteritis, but literally fatal errors resulted in her death.

Her parents, Mac and Neville Crawford, from Station Road, Letterbreen were, naturally, devastated by the little girl's death in April 2000. Compounding their agony was the fact that they felt frustrated by authority at every turn in their bid to find out why she died.

It has emerged that her death was not only preventable, but it was fundamental errors in her treatment that directly led to her death.

But it wasn't until this week that the man with overall responsibility for the running of the hospital gave a clear indication that they were culpable.

In an exclusive interview with the Impartial Reporter, Mr Hugh Mills, Chief Executive of the Sperrin Lakeland Trust was questioned about the now discredited internal review of the case. Initially, the review heard a consultant's opinion that he could not give "an absolute explanation as to why Lucy's condition deteriorated rapidly."

It was only when a Coroner's inquest in February heard another expert's opinion that the real cause of Lucy's death was revealed to the public. That a wrong dose of the wrong fluid was dripped into Lucy.

I asked Mr Mills "Is the Trust now prepared to acknowledge that they were responsible for Lucy's death?"

Mr Mills said: "We have done that in litigation."

Question: "No, you have said you were not contesting liability which falls far short. Are you now acknowledging that the Trust is responsible for Lucy's death?"

Mr Mills: "Yes. In the context of the full picture of medical knowledge at the time."

Question: "You're saying the hospital killed that child?"

Mr Mills: "That's an emotive way to put it, you are looking for a headline..." Significantly, though, Mr Mills did not contradict my interpretation.

I also asked him if the Trust would now apologise to the Crawford family. He claimed that a letter of apology had already been sent to the family.

However, I pointed out that the family and many others believed what was said in the letter fell well short of an apology.

"A full apology was the intention," insisted the Chief Executive.

I asked Mr Mills: "The intention of the letter was to say, 'we're sorry for causing Lucy's death'?"

Mr Mills agreed.

The admission of liability and apology is a major step; but it is likely to be too little too late for the Crawford family. Indeed, they do not accept that the letter from Mr Mills was an apology.

The letter this month, after the inquest, said: "I am writing on behalf of the Trust to indicate our regret and apologies for the failings in our service at the time of Lucy's death in April 2000."

Neville Crawford said this week: "We have been to hell and back a mil-

We have been to hell and back a million times. We have been devastated as a family; we asked ourselves was it our fault? In a few short hours they threw Lucy's life away. And they still have not said sorry to us.

— Neville Crawford

A picture of Lucy Crawford when she was a year old.

Hospital's 'fundamental errors' led to baby death

(From page one)

A 17-month-old baby admitted to the Erne Hospital with an upset stomach and dehydration died because of "fundamental errors" in the drip treatment she was given to replace the fluids she had lost through vomiting and diarrhoea.

Lucy Crawford, from Letterbreen, was given a "totally inappropriate" drip and the wrong dosage, failed to notice the "alarm bells" at her sodium levels fell rapidly and she developed a condition known as hyponatraemia. She died from swelling of the brain.

Nobody knows how many children have died as a result of hyponatraemia.

At Lucy's inquest this week questions were raised about the number of "other fatalities uncovered deaths across the UK" and in particular about whether an earlier examination of the circumstances of Lucy's death could have saved the life of one-

year-old Raychel Ferguson. She died 14 months later at Altnagelvin Hospital in Derry.

The coroner, Mr. John Leckey, called upon an expert, Dr. Edward Sumner, a consultant paediatric anaesthetist, "to investigate Raychel's death. He also asked Dr Sumner to produce an independent report on Lucy's death.

Dr. Sumner gave evidence that he had carefully examined the medical and nursing notes from the Erne. In his opinion Lucy died from acute swelling of the brain.

He said it was difficult to know how dehydrated she was when she was admitted to the Erne but on balance he thought she was mildly dehydrated, perhaps less than five per cent.

Dr. Sumner said it was "good practice" to record fluid levels to get a dismal view of the level of dehydration. In Lucy's case this was only done afterwards.

"What is absolutely mandatory is to write a full

prescription saying what fluid is to be given and at what rates. This was not done," he stated.

He said the prescription should be recorded on that patient's chart so that staff have clear and specific instructions.

He said Dr. O'Donohoe thought Lucy was getting 30 millilitres a hour when she was in fact getting 100 millilitres.

He described the type of drip solution given to her as "totally inappropriate", to replace the fluid she had lost and maintain her levels.

"I think Lucy effectively died in the Erne Hospital and I think the cause of death was acute cerebral oedema," he told the coroner.

In Dr. Sumner's opinion the underlying cause was hyponatraemia arising from the intravenous fluid treatment. He said acute gastroenteritis must have been a contributing factor.

Dr. Sumner said that, apart from a few small differences, his findings were in agreement with those of three other doctors who examined the case.

He was asked if he was aware of other children having died as a result of poor fluid management.

He replied: "I know several other cases where this was a very likely part of the mortality."

The court heard that the death of Raychel Ferguson, 14 months after Lucy, led to the drawing up of a protocol to remind doctors and medical staff of the potential risk of hyponatraemia to children on drips.

He agreed with a suggestion from Mr. Brian Fee, a barrister representing the Crawford family, that the wrong fluid was given at the wrong rate.

"I think they were both fundamental errors," he stated.

Mr. Fee asked if the combination of these two fundamental errors put Lucy on a course for catastrophe, and that catastrophe even occurred while she was still at the Erne Hospital.

"Yes," replied Dr. Sumner.

Mr. Fee suggested that at least a third fundamental error was made when Lucy's drip was changed to a normal saline solution and it was allowed to flow freely.

Dr. Sumner said free flow solution should not be given to children.

"What should never be allowed to happen," be stated, "in his opinion is only

exacerbated the situation.

Dr. Peter Crean, a consultant paediatric anaesthetist at the Royal Belfast Hospital for Sick Children, gave evidence that Lucy was admitted to the Erne in the early hours of Thursday, April 13, 2000, and died the following day.

The coroner asked if Lucy was a "very, very ill way child" when she arrived at the hospital and what the prognosis was.

Dr. Crean replied, "No, there was really no chance."

He said that when she was admitted to the Erne her sodium reading was fine and was within normal limits but by 3am had dropped to a low" 127. His cause for concern was the rate at which had dropped.

"It would certainly ring alarm bells," he stated.

Before leaving the Erne her pupils were dilated and unresponsive.

"That indicated some form of catastrophic event in the brain. I certainly felt the situation was not retrievable at that time," he stated.

He pointed out that there was often little warning that something adverse was happening to a child and that their condition can deteriorate very rapidly.

"Managing young children like this can be very difficult," he stressed.

"I think if Lucy's fluid had been managed in a different way maybe the outcome would have been different" said Dr. Crean.

Mr. Fee, instructed by Mr. Kevin Murnaghan, expressed the gratitude of the Crawford family to Dr. Crean and the medical staff at the Royal for the "professional and compassionate way" they were dealt with.

Mr. Fee suggested that the wrong fluid was given to Lucy.

Dr. Crean said it was wrong in that it was difficult to use one fluid generally in order to reduce the risk of hyponatraemia fluids should be tailored to meet the needs of the individual patient and their progress should be monitored. He suggested the use of two fluids, one as normal losses and the other to maintain levels, would have been more appropriate.

Mr. Fee suggested that Lucy was given the wrong dosage.

Dr. Crean replied he would have managed things differently and "I would agree that it was on the high side.

Third, it was wrong to allow free-flow and fourth, to use both maintenance and replacement."

The inquest continues.

Insight programme into child deaths wins top television award

The UTV programme which led to the setting up of an inquiry into the death of Fermanagh baby, Lucy Crawford has won the media industry's top award for journalism.

The team behind the Insight programme, "When Hospitals Kill" broadcast in October last year, was in London last week to receive the Royal Television Society's "National and Regional Current Affairs Programme of the Year" award. The judges said the programme had "not only made an impact – it made a difference". It's the first time in that UTV has ever won the award.

"When Hospitals Kill" was the result of several months of investigation by former Impartial Reporter journalist, Trevor Birney and producer, Ruth O'Reilly. The programme produced evidence of how the Sperrin Lakeland Trust had covered-up the death of little Lucy Crawford, daughter of Neville and Mac, who live at Letterbreen.

Lucy, aged 17-months, died after being admitted to the Erne Hospital in April, 2000. A Coroner found that the hospital's fluid management had killed her, Coroner John Leckey said that Lucy had received too much of the wrong fluid. Yet, "When Hospitals Kill" found that the management at the Sperrin Lakeland Trust had covered-up the fact that the Erne Hospital caused the death. The programme also discovered that doctors at the Royal Belfast Hospital for Sick Children had misled the Coroner into believing that Lucy's death was due to natural causes.

Following the broadcast of the programme, Health Minister, Angela Smyth appointed one of Northern Ireland's most respected barristers, John O'Hara QC, to set up an inquiry into the death of Lucy and two other children, Adam Strain and Raychel Ferguson, who also died from fluid mismanagement. The inquiry sat for the first time last month when John O'Hara announced that he was to add a fourth, as yet unnamed, death to his inquiry. It's understood that the QC is also considering investigating the death of another child, Conor Mitchell, which was also featured in the UTV programme.

In making the award, the Royal Television Society's judges praised the programme makers, stating:

"This was a careful, thorough and coherent investigation into often complicated and sensitive subject matter. The programme making team sustained interest throughout with imaginative production techniques – a difficult task with a story such as this which was buried in paperwork. The Judges said that the winning programme not only made an impact – it actually made a difference."

UTV's Director of Television, Alan Bremner said the award was as much about the efforts of the children's parents to get at the truth as the work of the journalists involved.

"This award recognises the courageous campaign fought by the parents of Adam, Lucy, Raychel and Conor to make Northern Ireland's health service accountable. I would also like to pay tribute to our Insight team for their tenacity and integrity in producing this programme," he said.

Trevor Birney, from Enniskillen worked in the Impartial Reporter before leaving to join Downtown Radio in 1994. He joined UTV in 1998 and become its Editor of Current Affairs three years ago. Ruth O'Reilly is originally from County Down and worked previously for the "Irish News" and the "Press Association."

Established 1825 — Thursday, 19th February, 2004

Mum blames hospital Trust for baby's death

* by Chris Donegan

Her body twitched, her eyes were flickering, her body rigid and I noticed that her hands were clenching backwards and tight fisted

A mother whose 17-month-old baby girl died after medical staff at the Erne Hospital made "fundamental errors" in her treatment has blamed the Sperrin Lakeland Health and Social Care Trust for her daughter's death.

Mrs. Mae Crawford, from Station Road, Lettербreen, also accuses the Trust of attempting to "brush Lucy's death under the carpet".

Baby Lucy Crawford had gastroenteritis, an acute viral infection of the stomach and intestine which caused her to vomit and gave her diarrhoea. As a result she became dehydrated. It was when she was admitted to the Erne and put on a drip to replace the fluids she had lost that fatal mistakes were made. Staff failed to properly manage her fluid level and she died from the resulting swelling of her brain.

The court heard that "fundamental errors" lead to her death. The wrong type of drip fluid was used and the wrong dose was given. Staff also failed to follow "good practice" in that they failed to keep records including the "absolutely mandatory" writing down of clear and specific instructions as to what drip was to be used and at what rates.

Lessons were not learned. Just over a year later a nine-year-old girl died in the Altnagelvin Hospital in Derry. As a result of her death a protocol was issued advising medical staff of the potential risks to children on drips, pointing out that the consequences can be extremely serious.

Mrs. Crawford gave evidence that Lucy was born at the Erne on November 5, 1998. On Tuesday, April 11, 2000, she became ill and vomited. She was taken to see her GP, Dr. Graham, at Enniskillen Health Centre. He examined her and said he could see nothing wrong and there was nothing to worry about.

However, the following evening Lucy was running a temperature so her parents took her to the Westdoc

Out of Hours surgery on the Tempo Road in Enniskillen where she was examined by Dr. Aisling Kirby, from Derrylin. Dr. Kirby advised them to take Lucy to the Erne as she was low on fluid and needed a drip. She assured them there was nothing to worry about.

Lucy was admitted to the Children's Ward around 7.20pm and was examined by Dr. Malik. He mentioned that there was a lot of gastroenteritis around. He looked for veins in Lucy's hands and foot and tried unsuccessfully 11 times to get an intravenous line inserted.

Mrs. Crawford said she expressed concerns because Lucy was not responding. She asked for blood tests to be carried out but was told by staff Nurse Brid Swift that the laboratory was closed and it would be morning before any tests would be checked.

Dr. O'Donohoe arrived and inserted a drip into Lucy's right hand. It was approximately 10.30pm.

Around 11pm Lucy was still not responding and was staring blankly. Her mother asked Dr. Malik to check her eyes. He shone a pen light into them and said she was OK.

"That was the last time Lucy was seen by a doctor until 3am," stated Mrs. Crawford.

Around 12.15am Lucy became a little restless and was sick. Mrs. Crawford cleaned her up and she fell asleep.

At 2.15am Lucy had a bowel movement which "frightened" her mother. It was runny, green and foul

smelling. Nurse Teresa McCaffrey said they would move her into a side ward because of the risk of infection to other patients.

Just before 3am Lucy moaned and started to breathe loudly.

"Her body twitched, her eyes were flickering, her body rigid and I noticed that her hands were clenching backwards and tight fisted. I called her by name and tried to open her hands but could not. I rang the bell but no-one came. I left the side ward and shouted up the ward," explained Mrs. Crawford.

"I lifted Lucy but she did not respond to me," she added.

Dr. Malik, Dr. O'Donohoe and a Dr. Anderson, a consultant anaesthetist, came into the room. They did not seem to have the necessary equipment to hand to treat Lucy. Nurses ran to get the equipment but did not seem to know what Dr. Anderson was looking for.

"Dr. Anderson was obviously frustrated and said he needed a smaller line. He then, in no uncertain terms, told me to get out of the room," said Mrs. Crawford.

At 3.35am Sister Edmundson told them they were moving Lucy to the Intensive Care Ward.

Around 5.30am a nurse came and told them Lucy was being transferred to the Royal Belfast Hospital for Sick Children. They asked if their daughter could be air lifted to the Royal but were told this did not happen.

Around 6.40am Dr. O'Donohoe

> *I called her by name and tried to open her hands but could not. I rang the bell but no-one came. I left the side ward and shouted up the ward*

and a nurse left with Lucy in an ambulance for Belfast. Mrs. Crawford was not allowed to travel with her. She and her husband went in their own car.

At 10am the doctors at the Royal spoke to them and said Lucy's condition was very serious.

"They did not give us any hope. They said that they could do nothing with a dead baby," stated Mrs. Crawford.

She said Dr. Peter Crean expressed "anger and frustration" that Lucy's notes had still not arrived from Enniskillen.

The following day, Friday, April 14, they were told that brain stem tests had proved negative and there was no alternative but to take Lucy off the ventilator. She was taken off the ventilator at 1pm.

Mrs. Crawford said they met with Dr. O'Donohoe a month later but he was unable to answer their questions about Lucy's death. They then complained to the Sperrin Lakeland Health and Social Care Trust. They subsequently received a letter from the Trust stating that "the outcome of our review has not suggested that the care provided to Lucy was inadequate or of poor quality."

Mrs. Crawford continued: "Looking back we feel we were not listened to and side-lined in every way. It always seemed that everyone was avoiding the most important issue: What happened to Lucy? As of today we still have not received an explanation from the Sperrin Lakeland Health and Social Care Trust or any of its employees as to what did happen to Lucy or what caused her death.

"We are all human, mistakes are made, apologies are given and appropriate measures are put in place to ensure such events never recur. Instead we feel the Sperrin Lakeland Health and Social Care Trust have tried to brush Lucy's death under the carpet.

"We feel our little girl, Lucy, was totally let down by the Sperrin Lakeland Health and Social Care Trust. Lucy had been placed in their care and they were responsible for her. We feel that the acts and omissions of the Trust caused Lucy's death. We feel that the acts and omissions of the Trust since Lucy's death have caused us greater pain and suffering. The Trust has not been able to deal appropriately with the consequences of Lucy's death. In this instance what is supposed to be the 'caring profession' have in my book become the 'uncaring' profession," she added.

She said Lucy's death had had a "profound, debilitating and devastating effect" on the family.

"Lucy was a very special little girl and important member of our family. We miss her terribly.

"I wish it to be made known that I hold the Sperrin Lakeland Health and Social Care Trust wholly accountable and fully responsible for Lucy's death," stated Mrs. Crawford.

• *Continued on page two*

A senior doctor has blamed the former Minister of Health for creating the uncertainty which led staff to leave the Erne Hospital and the problems which put critically ill patients at risk.

Dr. Mahen Varma, consultant cardiologist at the Erne, said Sinn Fein's Bairbre de Bruin allowed the siting of the new acute hospital for the south-west to become a "political football." He said the uncertainty created staff shortages which left medical teams "stretched to the maximum" and "unintentional mistakes" being made.

Reacting to the findings of the Risk and Governance Review of Acute Hospital Services, he acknowledged: "It's a damning report, I have to say that, but we can move forward from it and in moving forward it will hopefully improve the services. But we have to ask ourselves: 'How has this arisen?' And the answer to that is very simple. The Minister of Health in 2001, Bairbre de Bruin, when she got the Hayes recommendation(that the new acute hospital to serve the south-west should be in Enniskillen), became a political football between politicians in Enniskillen and Omagh as to the siting of the new hospital. She did not have the political will to implement it.

"This delay by lack of political direction and decision-making led to the fact that recruitment of staff in both hospitals(Erne and Tyrone County) became very difficult because of the uncertainty over the siting of the new hospital, hence the staff that were present were stretched to the maximum and with the best will in the world nurses and doctors can only do so much, because they're also human, and under these circumstances unintentional mistakes will be made.

"The fault here is lack of decision making by the Minister of Health, and in two meetings I had with the Minister I pointed out the issues including those of clinical governance, which has been highlighted in this report. Since the Hayes Report came out we have lost anaesthetists, we have lost surgeons and we have lost nurses, and as a result of that we have been understaffed and we have had to rely on locum cover and agency nurses. If a decision had been made four years ago that the new hospital was going to be in Enniskillen and they had got on with it I don't think we would have lost staff," said Dr. Varma.

He pointed out that hospital management, the Sperrin Lakeland Trust, has been to Poland to recruit anaesthetists and surgeons who are now working here full time.

He said he was not going to get involved in the blame game.

"It would not be right to criticise any one member of the Trust Board," he stated.

Asked if medical staff had reported incidents and mistakes, he replied: "The bulk of the incidents that are alluded to in the report would appear to have taken place in Omagh. Any difficulties that took place at this site, we did point out to management.

"Any shortcomings I was aware of as a clinician, I brought to the attention of the administration. Occasionally it wasn't acted upon. They were not incidents of a critical or life-threatening nature," he emphasised.

Asked about the death of Lucy Crawford, Dr. Varma said: "I was not aware of that until I read about it in your paper."

He continued: "I should also point out that I have spoken to a number of colleagues

> **" I should also point out that I have spoken to a number of colleagues from other hospitals in Northern Ireland and what has transpired in the Sperrin Lakeland Trust is not unique "**

from other hospitals in Northern Ireland and what has transpired in the Sperrin Lakeland Trust is not unique.

"Where we go from here is simple. There is an action plan, as I understand it, to address the issues highlighted in the report and already guidelines have been laid down about the patients in intensive care," he explained.

He called up those guidelines on his computer screen, pointing out that they were issued last Friday, the day after the damning report was made public.

Can patients have confidence in the Erne?

"No nurse or doctor wants to intentionally harm patients. It's their intention at all times - working with them as I have

for well over 20 years in this hospital - that they wish to provide the best and highest quality of care that is available," said Dr. Varma.

"Whilst I accept this report shows the Trust in a very bad light we must all approach the report in the spirit of learning from the past and as a source of ideas for improving the protection of patients in the future. It does not mean services in the hospital are like that all the time and certainly as a result of the new Health Minister, Shaun Woodward's edict, changes are already in place so there is no reason they shouldn't get the highest level of care. In any one year there are thousands of patients that go through the two hospitals that are very well looked after. If there was any degree of negligence in the normal day-to-day running of the hospital then all areas of the hospital would come under investigation," he added.

"Now that the Minister has acted in a decisive way it's my hope he will now be pro-active in instructing all his staff to try and get the new hospital up and running as soon as possible so that incidents highlighted in the report will not recur," stated Dr. Varma.

Thursday, 16th June, 2005

Confidential papers: Department knew Health Trust was in trouble

by Dearil McDaniel

It has emerged that the Department of Health became aware of major concerns over patients in the Erne Hospital at least a year ago.

Details have been made public of confidential meetings the Department held with the Sperrin Lakeland Trust in 2004 in which they refer to concerns over three deaths. In four hospitals in two of the deaths, Trust officials were "unsure" if post mortems had been carried out and whether or not they had been reported to the Chief Medical Officer.

At least two of the deaths are known to have happened in the Erne.

The revelations are among hundreds of previously unpublished documents passed to the O'Hara inquiry.

John O'Hara is holding an inquiry into hyponatraemia-related deaths, including that of Lucy Crawford.

Mr O'Hara is to hold a public hearing in Belfast next week, described as a "progress report".

And this morning, (Thursday) the Sperrin Lakeland Trust moves for the first time since Hugh Mills was forced to resign over a report which showed alarming shortcomings in Trust management.

The Trust has appointed an interim Chief Executive, Mr Fred Fielk, and today the board has allocated 45 minutes to discuss its Lewis report which highlighted the risk to patients in hospitals run by the Trust.

In advance of this written evidence sent to the O'Hara is beginning to give some more insight into how deep the problems were.

In April last year, weeks after the Lucy Crawford inquest, Department of Health officials met privately with Trust officials, including Hugh Mills and Eugene Fee.

One document, marked "Confidential Sperrin Lakeland Trust" has notes of a number of meetings.

On April 23, part of it says "Discussed issues surrounding the Lucy Crawford case. ... Asked if there were any other issues within the Trust that may have cause for concern. Advised there had been a

maternal death (a member of staff) potential issue of not having transferred the mother to another unit earlier as this was a premature birth. Asked if the CMO (Chief Medical Officer) had been made aware of this incident in light of the fact of the Lucy Crawford case. Both were unaware and advised that perhaps they should inform the CMO.

The document also refers to a meeting in June last year with Margaret Kelly, director of nursing with the Western Board, although it does not say who else was present.

A note states: "Have concerns with Sperrin Lakeland that are wider than the Lucy Crawford issue. Also now aware of a maternal death and with patient safety issues in Anaesthetics."

A series of notes are taken throughout the month of June which show contact between senior health officials in various sections, such as Ian Carson, (Deputy Chief Medical Officer), the Clinical and Social Care Governance Support Team and the Department itself.

One note says: "Telephone call from Dr Ian Carson (DCMO), Andrew Hamilton (Deputy Secretary) came to see him with concerns about the Trust."

And the document shows on July 14: "Discussed with CMO and DCMO re Sperrin Lakeland. Concerns about two other cases that have recently come to light.

1. Man aged 23 – died. Cause – unsure of whether case was referred to Coroner or if PM (post mortem) was carried out.

2. Child aged 7 who was admitted with ***** Child subsequently died. Unsure if PM was carried out. CMO informed of death two days ago. Both incidents occurred around two years ago."

Although these incidents are on the inquiry website and, therefore, in the public domain, the Impartial Reporter has taken out some of the details which may identify the people locally.

As the document goes on, it shows that Hugh Mills received a letter last June from paediatricians in the Trust expressing concern about nursing staffing levels.

By September, officials were expressing concern about the Sperrin Lakeland Trust's

handling of the the "Root Cause Analysis" review of Lucy Crawford's death.

This review was being publicly backed by the then Health Minister, Angela Smith, but the document on the website reveals: "Wednesday 15th September Telephone discussion with Dean Sullivan (Director of Secondary Care). He is not aware of why Sperrin Lakeland have decided to change looking at the L.C. case. Unhappy if this was to be the case."

Hugh Mills was later offered some "communication facilitation" but told the officials he needed to discuss this with Bridget O'Rawe (Trust Director of Corporate Affairs), and in October a handwritten note says "Meeting with Hugh Mills. Discussed offer of communications sessions for SLT Didn't appear keen to accept offer."

Although the Department was aware in June about safety issues in Anaesthetics, it was November before the review group was set up. It was this report, eventually damning and forced the resignation of Hugh Mills.

Documents on the inquiry website show the Department was deeply involved in discussion over the competence of the Trust throughout 2004.

Yet in another section of the website briefings for the Minister, Ms Smith show officials from another part of the Ministry advising her to tell the press "I am satisfied that the Trust investigated the (Lucy Crawford) case properly and I see no reason for the Chief Executive to resign."

In fact, not only has Mr Mills been forced to resign over the damning Lewis report, but a number of other figures referred to in correspondence are no longer in their posts. Trust director, Mr Eugene Fee has retired early, and this week the Department of Health confirmed that Permanent Secretary, Mr Clive Gowdy is retiring early on health grounds.

Two members of the press department, Mr Kevin Mulhern and Mr Colm Shannon have also moved from the Department of Health.

These departures are referred to further in our story on page 4.